# THINKING HABITS FOR DEFINITE SUCCESS

SIMPLE WAYS TO ACHIEVE YOUR GOALS BY
CHANGING YOUR HABITS OF THINKING

ROMA SHARMA

FIRST EDITION, SELF-PUBLISHED BY ROMA SHARMA
PRINTED IN INDIA

ISBN 978-93-5426-422-1

# DISCLAIMER

This book is for informational purposes only. The views expressed are those of the author alone and should be implemented by the reader at his/her own responsibility. The information provided is of a general nature only. Stories, examples and anecdotes provided in this book are fictional and any resemblance to a person or situation is purely coincidental.

The author does not intend to imply any particular problem or situation to be related specifically to the male gender or the female one. The gender neutrality of the characters needs to be maintained on part of the reader and the context needs to be seen irrespective of the gender being used.

Adherence to all applicable laws and regulations including international, federal, state and local governing professional licensing, business practices, advertising and all other aspects of doing business in any jurisdiction is the sole responsibility of the reader or purchaser. Neither the author nor the publisher assumes any responsibility or liability whatsoever on the behalf of the purchaser or reader of these materials.

# CONTENTS

# THINKING HABITS FOR DEFINITE SUCCESS: AN INTRODUCTION

What makes one person highly effective in producing results while another struggles to do the same? We have seen people with the bare minimum resources reaching phenomenal heights and others, who had everything going for them, unable to generate the results they wanted. If people succeed despite unconducive circumstances, then it is something inside their minds that helped them get there. In this book, we will explore what that is in depth.

At the time of writing, I have been working as a coach and trainer for over six years. Working closely with clients towards achieving their goals has given me the opportunity to observe the thinking patterns of top performers. My biggest takeaway is that it does not matter which field the person is from. The goal doesn't matter either. It is the thought process that gets them the result they want. I might be coaching clients who want to increase their income, improve their public speaking skills, develop better relationships, or become fit. The mental patterns that are effective in achieving those results are the same. The forces that they tussle with are the same as well, like the fear of failure, fear of uncertainty, or lack of faith in one's abilities which causes them to procrastinate—put things off for another day—a day which never comes.

The people who achieve their goals take their challenges head-on. They have positive beliefs about who they are and what they deserve. Setbacks—that inevitably come with pursuing goals—don't bother them. They are action-oriented and determined. They have specific ways of interpreting results that keep them motivated during tough times. It's not that they don't experience fear, but they do what they must anyway.

A plan can always be created to meet outcomes. What matters is what you do with the plan. Let's say a person wants to get fit. She can make a diet chart and a daily exercise routine. She can create a foolproof plan to regain her fitness, but the knowledge isn't enough. If she doesn't take any action, she won't get any results. If she doesn't believe in her plan, the fact that she acted upon it might not help her either. It's not about what you know, it's about what you do—inside your mind and outside, in real life. Both are important and interconnected.

The same applies to a person who wants to have good relationships. In my business coaching sessions, I go considerably over interpersonal issues. If your goal is to improve your relationships—whether at the workplace or at home—you might need to start with your beliefs about the people in your environment. Discussing the content of the problem is not helpful. The solution lies in the pattern of thinking.

In this book you will discover:

1.  Simple frames of thinking that can transform your results.
2.  Beliefs of excellence observed in highly successful people.
3.  The Self-fulfilling prophecy—how you create things by thinking about them.
4.  Powerful self-coaching tools to define your goals and eliminate roadblocks.
5.  Practical ways to quit procrastination and stay motivated during challenging times.
6.  Steps to alter thinking habits incrementally and build a strong success mindset.

The recommendations provided in this book are based on the work I have done with my clients over the years. Hence, it is strictly information that has been tried and tested—and works! Exercises have been provided at the end of each section to help you define your goals, remove roadblocks, and be successful.

While reading this book, please keep your goals—personal or professional—in mind. These simple yet powerful thought patterns bring tremendous success when adopted into one's daily life. I hope you are as excited to get started as I am.

Do you also want to discover the 7 best ways to be yourself confidently and unapologetically? In Roma's book, **"What Will People Think?"** you will find a complete guide to stop caring about what others think.

# Also By Roma

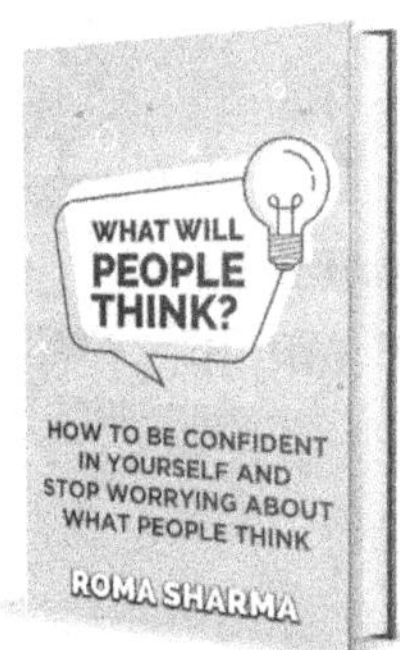


What readers say about "What Will People Think?":

"This book has all the elements one needs to succeed"
"This book helped me get rid of my limiting beliefs"
"A simple, easy read with lots of examples I can
relate to"

**Log onto romasharma.com** and buy your copy of **"What Will People Think?"** today.

2.  Affirmations to increase self-esteem and confidence

3.  Self-coaching questions that will help you find solutions in difficult situations

4.  Simple ways to decrease worry and stay calm in the present moment

While reading the book, **Thinking Habits For Definite Success**, please refer to the self-coaching questions in the **Being Yourself Journal** for best results.

**Download now! Log onto romasharma.com**

## WHAT IS SUCCESS?

What is success to you? What has to happen for you to feel successful?

In my coaching sessions, I work with my clients to define their goals. I have noticed that the way people represent success to themselves is subjective. Some people take the monetary angle to success. They feel like they have succeeded only when they earn a certain amount of money. There are others who don't have a fixed amount of money in mind. They feel successful as long as they are earning more than their acquaintances. Then there are people who want an esteemed position in their jobs. Their title defines their level of success.

Due to the nature of my work, I know quite a few therapists and coaches personally. Some of them have goals in terms of the number of people they want to help. They work with organizations that provide free counseling. Recently, I met one such therapist who said that she would feel successful if she provided counseling support to at least 500 people in her career span.

It's interesting to see how the definition of success differs—one person wants a million dollars while another wants her to be of service to others.

It is difficult to give a blanket definition to the word *success*. Going forward, we will refer to it as anything a person set out to achieve and did. It will also include how achieving the goal impacted the person overall. If a person earned all that she wanted to but became impatient and temperamental while doing so, she might not be successful after all. If she met her monetary goals at the expense of personal relationships, we can't call it success either. It would be like striving to climb a mountain only to realize that there is no one to share the view with.

*Goals can be achieved one way or another. The question is, what are you becoming in the process?*

Success is when a goal is achieved while promoting the overall wellbeing of the person—physically, mentally, and emotionally. Along with money, name, or fame we strive towards, we also need the health to enjoy it. Without that, other achievements aren't of much use.

2

___

## THINKING IS A HABIT

Have you noticed that your habits strengthen over time? You become great at anything you do repeatedly. Be it physical exercise (like swimming, cycling, cooking) or mental exercise (like thinking, imagining, or remembering).

Mostly when we think we are *thinking,* we are actually *remembering.* Thinking burns metabolic energy, tires us out. We default to memories of similar situations and mimic them in action, even if it did not work well for us! It's easier for us to recall and repeat than to think and act differently.

*Thinking is a deliberate activity, whereas remembering is a default activity.*

Experiments conducted to analyze brain scans have indicated that the parts of the brain that light up when a person is thinking are the same as the parts that light up when a person is in pain. We might not be physically experiencing pain, however, the energy burn out becomes clear to us when we examine specific scenarios. For instance, have you noticed how tiring it is to do something for the first time? It requires thinking, since you don't have any memory to fall back on. Your brain strains to create new neural pathways for the activity. The pain associated with this much thinking is one reason we avoid doing new things. The intensity of pain reduces when we perform the task for a second time and, furthermore, the subsequent times.

First-time activity thin neural strand created (thinking causes pain)

Repeated activity more neural strands created (remembering makes it easier)

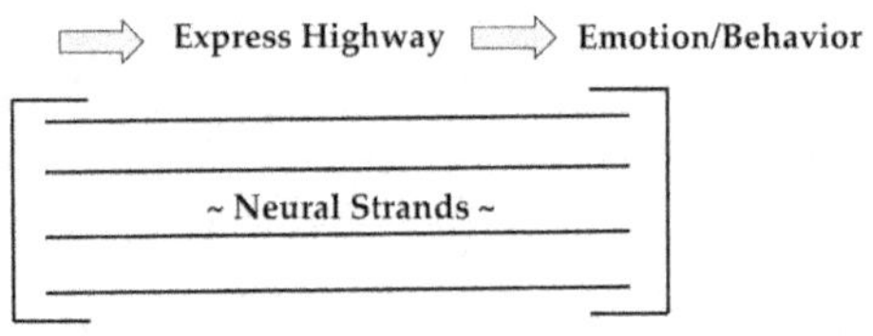


Repetition Strengthens the Pattern
of Emotion/Behavior

We can imagine neural pathways as wiring in the brain. If you indulge in any thinking pattern repeatedly, the neural pathways get strengthened to the point that they become an express highway to that emotion or behavior. Many such strengthened neural pathways result in thinking on autopilot. We don't stop to ask ourselves if the current situation is the same as it was the last time. Has anything changed or can we do something better? We unconsciously avoid thinking, which causes repeated behaviors. This creates a future that resembles our past.

David was a talented team manager at a product-based company. He had recently shifted to a new team and his subordinates knew more about the work than him. Being in a leadership position, he had to pick up the required skills quickly to guide them in the right direction. Thankfully, he had a helpful peer called Mike, another project manager.

David struggled to understand his new team's performance. He reviewed the production line, analyzed their spreadsheets, and went over the previous years' reports. The number of things he had to learn overwhelmed him. He wondered how Mike could do so with such ease. Gradually, over a few months of hard work, David became efficient at managing his team. He did not need Mike's help anymore. He was happy with his progress.

At the end of the year, David's manager, Chris, invited him and Mike to discuss their performance so far. He told them that while they had been running their teams efficiently, there had been no improvement in their methods for a few years. There were newer, cheaper tools in the market to help them optimize their cost of production. Hiring more qualified people could improve their overall productivity as well.

David viewed Chris as a person who was never happy with anything he did. He perceived his advice as rejection and did not pay heed to it. Mike challenged David's thought process, pointing out that he was remembering the times Chris was unhappy with them, rather than pondering upon his words. This made David take a long, hard look at how he was running the team. He chalked out a plan to improve their methods and produce tangible results in a few months.

David and Mike were not thinking about improving team efficiency until Chris pointed it out. They might have struggled to learn the ropes, but once they did, they got comfortable. They knew what worked and what did not and ran the team habitually. The way David viewed Chris was also habitual. Testing the current situation—independent of past impressions—would require David to think. That is what he did when Mike challenged his thought process.

*We are a result of whatever we have been practicing. Breaking out of our thinking habits requires an interrupt!*

If we shout at someone today, we are twice as likely to shout at someone again tomorrow and three times as likely the following day. Our neurology gets conditioned to generate responses automatically. If we are in a habit of finding fault, blaming people or worrying, over time we become better at it—whether we like it or not.

What can we do, given that we have already set several neural strands as thinking habits? Can we change the wiring of our brains? I'm glad to tell you that we can. Stay with me as we go deeper into the best ways of changing our mindsets for success.

# 3

## YOUR TWO MINDS

Think of a time when you set a goal for yourself, put a plan in action and nailed it! What was your state of mind at the time?

Now think of a time when you really wanted something. You put a plan in action but were unsuccessful. Do you remember how you had felt while you were executing your plan? Pause, take a deep breath, and shake off the feeling. Return to the book when you are ready.

What was the difference between the two situations you revisited? Focus on the feeling states. Wasn't the way you felt about your goal and the possibility of achieving it different for when you were successful and when you were not?

It does not matter if you are running for the gold in the Olympics, restoring a lost relationship, working towards a promotion, or trying to have a tough conversation—everything is possible with the right state!

The feelings that support success are subjective to an individual—one might need to feel happy, excited, or confident to perform well, while another might need to feel peaceful or relaxed. The important question is, what feelings help *you* generate your results?

Thoughts result in feelings, and feelings result in behavior. The act of being successful is just visible behavior. However, if you do not back this behavior with a feeling that supports it, the act does not take place at all. This happens because of the tussle between the two minds that drive you—the conscious and the unconscious mind.

> Please note: people sometimes refer to the **unconscious mind** as the **subconscious mind**. This book refers to them synonymously.

At this moment, you are reading this book or paying attention to something in your environment using your conscious mind, which runs only 10% of your behavior. It is the least informed and the last to know about anything. It comes up with two reasons for your actions —one, the reason you give other people, and two, the real reason. The conscious mind talks loudly in the foreground. You can hear it as the voice in your head. (It's the same one that just said, "What voice?")

The unconscious mind is your body, which communicates with you via feelings and runs 90% of your behavior. Its primary function is keeping you safe, even at the cost of happiness. It is highly intelligent and runs your body with no conscious effort on your part—it keeps your heart rate in check; regulates your body temperature; keeps your lungs working and ensures that your system is functioning, whether you are sleeping or awake. It communicates with you in the form of feelings and has the emotional age of a child.

*Your feelings primarily come from your unconscious mind and can be felt in your body.*

As you continue to read this book, if your mind wanders, visits a person, place, or situation, it is happening inside your unconscious mind. You might have noticed that you may be happily engaged in an activity, and out of the blue you remember something that throws you off balance. This is an example of the unconscious mind communicating with you. It is charged with emotions and can get you to do anything. It can also generate emotions that can keep you from doing the things you want to do.

Unlike the conscious mind, the unconscious mind whispers softly in the background. It knows intuitively when something is not right for you. Hence, it is important to pay attention to your feelings, otherwise it is like ignoring the signals on the dashboard while flying a plane.

Imagine you were to tell yourself consciously, "I am going to land on the moon someday," and there is this icky feeling inside you which softly says, "No, you can't." This is the feeling to watch out for, the one that stops you from getting what you want. We might consciously tell ourselves that we are going to earn a million dollars, reach our ideal weight, or travel the world, but as long as the unconscious mind contradicts it, we cannot.

*To be successful in our goals, our conscious mind needs to align with our unconscious mind.*

The thought (in the conscious mind) needs to be backed with a feeling (in the unconscious mind) that supports it. When that happens, we become unstoppable.

# 4

# CHANGING MINDSETS: ALIGNING THE TWO MINDS

Before working on a presenting problem, I ask my clients if they are ready to let go of it. As they answer, I pay more attention to their body language than their words. Sometimes they say, "Yes," but their non-verbal communication says, "No." In such cases, I work around the resistance towards solving the problem rather than solving the problem itself. The conscious and unconscious minds need alignment.

There are ways to align the two minds, and back our conscious thoughts with the desired unconscious feelings. Before doing so, we must check whether we want to align the minds or not. The unconscious mind has its reasons for creating unsupportive feelings.

Sometimes, it's just the comfort that comes with familiarity. When we do nothing different, there is no chance of going wrong, and we can remain free of problems, but, unfortunately, growth as well. Our unconscious mind is very protective of us. It protects us from pain, even if there are benefits to the pain, such as learning for the future. It is more concerned with our safety at present. Therefore, it prefers to maintain the status quo.

This comes from evolution, that is, our two-million-year-old reptilian brain. An animal does not go out of its way to set bigger goals. It does not voluntarily fight a larger group of animals or battle calamities for the sake of a reward. It would rather avoid a fight unless something important—like safety, food, or an opportunity to mate—is at stake. With similar instincts alive inside us, we experience fear when we try to give up our comfort zone in the hope of a better tomorrow.

It is possible to fight this instinct by using a power that only we have—the power of visualization. We have the ability to imagine how things will be. We can use this to our benefit, by linking pleasure to the imagination.

We gravitate naturally towards things we find pleasurable rather than those we find painful. While a task we are executing is giving us pain, we might lose sight of the pleasure we will experience if we power through the issues and emerge successful.

The *planner* and *doer* are two different states in our minds. The planner enjoys making plans, but the doer comes up with roadblocks that the planner might not have anticipated. As the challenges escalate, the initial motivation fizzles out, resulting in a delayed or abandoned project.

*It helps to leverage the joy of a successful task rather than dwell upon the difficulties of the present moment.*

When things don't go as planned, discouraging self-talk sounds like: "I am so sick of everything. I am constantly getting stuck with these issues. I can't handle it anymore."

The associated feeling can be changed instantly, by replacing it with more encouraging self-talk, such as: "My work has value because of the issues I fix. These issues have increased my level of competency and continue to do so. It will thrill me to resolve them successfully. The tougher the battle, the sweeter the victory… and mine is around the corner!"

Both these inner dialogues create diametrically opposite feelings. The first one keeps the person focused on the issues at hand, whereas the other highlights the benefits of resolving them. The thought process forms the basis for the feeling and the feeling forms the basis for the subsequent action.

**Exercise**

**Thought-Feeling-Action-Result (TFAR) Coaching Model**

Discover your thoughts and feelings for success.

**Case 1**: Think of a time when you set a plan in action and achieved what you set out to.

1. What were your feelings about the goal and the possibility of achieving it?
2. What specific actions did you take?
3. What were your feelings while taking those actions?
4. What was the result? How did you feel when you got that result?

**Case 2**: Think of a time when you set a plan in action and could not achieve what you wanted to. Answer the above questions again.

| Result | Action | Feeling | Thought |
|---|---|---|---|
| Case 1 | | | |
| Case 2 | | | |

TFAR Coaching Model

## Self-reflection:

1. What was the difference in feeling in Case 1 as opposed to Case 2?

2. What were your beliefs about the goal and your ability to achieve it?
3. If you were to pick the thoughts and feelings from Case 1 and map it onto Case 2, would that increase your chances of success in Case 2?

## No Pain, No Gain

If the *doer* in us talks encouragingly and accepts the pain of the current task as worth facing, it becomes easy for us to execute our plans. People rarely advocate the concept of accepting pain in the present. Social media bombards us with messages of instant gratification, such as-

*"Get rich quick, find out how."*

*"Double your income by working one hour a day."*

*"Doing this for 5 minutes can change your life forever."*

*"This one secret helped me shed 50 pounds without dieting or exercising."*

These videos and posts get a million clicks, which shows that there is a large section of viewers that like the concept of *something for nothing*. Advertisers use this to grab their attention. If the advertisement were to say that we need to work hard to earn money or that we had to exercise regularly to be fit, fewer people would be interested.

While doing things smartly achieves excellent results, the ones mentioned above are not smart solutions to problems. They are just clickbait, vying for our attention to meet their own targets. Social media platforms are useful, but not when we engage in concepts that serve us only in theory.

Let's look at anything awesome we may have achieved. It is invariably the result of a good plan, hard work, and some useful beliefs backing our efforts. Before setting a goal, we need to ask ourselves-

*"What am I willing to give up in order to get what I want?"*

This question assumes that it requires some resources to generate results. The answer to this question needs to be well-thought-out. Ensure what you are giving up is not something that will rock your boat. For instance, some people spend so much time pursuing their career goals that they don't find the opportunity to nurture important relationships. Eventually, they achieve their goals but are unhappy.

While you must give something up to get something else, the question is: *What?* Is it something more valuable to you than the goal you are pursuing? You need to choose the type of fuel and its quantity before revving up your engine, because once it is consumed, it cannot be retrieved.

## The Reason Behind Your Goal

We do nothing without a pay-off. Even if it's a simple, pleasurable activity, like watching television or speaking to a friend, we do it only when we get something in return, usually a feeling. When you connect with the reason behind your desire, it increases your chances of achieving it.

*Know the **why**, and the **how** will follow.*

Why might someone want more money? It's not as though the person wants to carry around bundles of paper. It's what that money represents—freedom, confidence or comfort. Why might a person want to be fit or get a better job? Perhaps because it represents a sense of wellbeing to the person.

While exploring the **why** you need to contemplate upon two factors which help in defining a goal:

## 1. A Goal Defined by Others

When people set their goals based on what someone else wants of them, they are not excited enough to follow through with their plans. They come up with excuses for not acting on their goals. For instance, there is a lady who does not want to take up a job. However, her husband wants her to find employment so she can support the finances of the house. She does not apply to any company, saying that she was too busy to do so. She might even believe her reason, but, subconsciously, she is not acting on the goal because she does not connect with it.

You might enjoy making others happy occasionally. However, it does not work out well in the long run if you set your goal involuntarily. When the going gets tough, you will either lose motivation, or feel like a victim, forced to do something for the sake of others.

*If your goal has a strong personal reason behind it, it becomes easier to stay motivated.*

This is one reason I'm careful while taking up clients whom someone else brings to me. Unless he or she is willing, the person being coached will not feel the need to work. Sometimes, parents ask me to coach their teenage children. I am happy to do so, but only if their children attend the session voluntarily. Otherwise, the parents' coaching goals will become mine, which could push the child further away, as the case may be.

## 2. A Goal as an Escape Route

Sometimes people create a goal to escape an uncomfortable situation. They decide to start their business venture, not because they want to, but because they are trying to escape the pain of a denied promotion. Couples decide to start a family, not because they want to have children, but because they want to escape resolving their marital issues.

Detecting whether one's goal is merely an escape is difficult, because it happens at an unconscious level. People are usually unaware of it unless someone challenges them. This darer may or may not come along. The best way to avoid this situation is to check explicitly with ourselves as to what achieving our goal will provide us at a deeper level.

5

**WELL-DEFINED OUTCOMES**

What if you were inside a dark room and had to hit an invisible target? Would you be able to? If you kept shooting randomly you might accidentally hit bullseye, but the chances are less. It will not be a result you could easily replicate either. However, if we switched on the lights and allowed you to take aim, you would stand a much better chance of hitting it.

The first step towards success is your ability to perceive your goal clearly. The clearer the goal is, the easier it becomes to pursue it. Before formalizing a goal, there are some important points to consider. We will go over each of them in the following sections.

**State the Goal in Positive Terms**

In my coaching sessions, I often hear people say that they don't want poor relationships or that they want to lose weight. While these outcomes have a positive intention, they need restructuring:

**1) Use positive terms**: A goal which starts with 'I don't want…' creates a negation in the mind. Our unconscious mind does not understand negatives. Let me explain this with an example. For the next step, I need you to not visualize an orange parrot. Whatever else you may think about, do not think about an orange parrot sitting on your shoulder. Try to do this for the next few minutes.

Did you notice that you started thinking about an orange parrot? But didn't I tell you *not to*? That is how our programming is. When someone says, "Don't look over there," we look in the suggested direction, despite being asked not to. Until negatively prompted, we might not have bothered to look, but now we are! Our unconscious mind could not process the *don't* and we only understood *look over there*.

Hence, instead of saying "I don't want to have poor relationships," we can state the goal in positive terms, such as, "I want to have good relationships." Instead of having a goal of losing weight—where *losing* is something our unconscious mind cannot understand—we can aim at becoming fit.

*Ensure that the goal is always something you **want** and not something you **don't want**. Your unconscious mind does not understand **don'ts**.*

**2) Be specific**: Once you have stated the goal in positive terms, you need to ensure that it is clear. Goals like, "I want to have good relationships," although stated positively, do not provide clarity on what a *good relationship* is, because *good* and *bad* are subjective experiences. You need to mention the specific person you want to improve your relationship with and how you would know that you have met your goal.

Certain goals are tangible. It helps to define them with metrics so you can measure the results. If you say that you want *more money,* it's unclear how much more. Hence, if your goal is to make more money, read more books, or reach a certain weight—set a number to it, say X.

Make the goal deadline sensitive. A loose deadline is as good as no deadline. It's important to have a date by when you would like to meet your goal. Let's say that date is Y.

We now have a measurable goal—we want X by Y.

I can write my objective as, "I want 100 more followers on my Facebook page by 31$^{st}$ December of the current year."

A vague goal like, "I want to get fit," can be replaced by how much you would like to weigh and by when. For instance, "I would like to weigh 150 pounds by 31$^{st}$ December of this year." Even an intangible goal, like improving a relationship, can have a deadline. That will concretize the goal.

Break bigger time periods into smaller ones. Have long-term goals, which will define where you would like to be 5 years and 10 years from now. Next, break the time periods into smaller frames like 1 year, 6 months, 3 months, etc. Well-defined short-term and long-term goals need periodic revision to check if you are on track. (Set your goals by using the question toolkit provided in the *'Being Yourself Journal'*. Download your free copy on romasharma.com)

**Evidence Procedure**

Specify your goal using sensory-based terms. What will you see, hear, and feel when you have achieved it? There are two benefits of doing so:

**1) The unconscious mind gets programmed**: You experience the world through your senses. It is inside your mind that you watch movies, hear voices, and talk to yourself—and this interplay creates your inner experience.

Whatever you experience strongly and tell yourself repeatedly will actualize itself. Using your imagination and self-talk, you can program your unconscious mind. The more your unconscious mind is engaged in the process of goal-definition, the higher is the chance that you will act on your goals.

**2) We have evidence of the goal being achieved**: How will you know that you have achieved your goal? Without a sensory-based definition, you might achieve your goal and not know it. Imagine, you met your fitness goal, but you didn't realize it because you didn't have a way to define your experience of success. Some of my clients imagine standing on a weighing scale and seeing a certain value on it or fitting into a dress. These representations help them realize that they have achieved their goal.

If your goal is to have a better relationship with someone, you might believe that you have achieved it when you feel calm or happy around this person. This definition is subjective to an individual and is usually feeling-based.

## Self-reflection:

1. What would things look like once you have achieved your goal?
2. What voices and sounds will you hear when your goal materializes?
3. How will you feel when that happens?

You might hear people cheering as you make your victory lap or see yourself in your brand-new cabin after your promotion. You might hear people congratulating you as well. Paint your picture as vividly as possible using sensorial information.

## Make it Compelling

If your goal does not draw you towards itself, you will most probably not do anything about it. You may start off enthusiastically, but your energy will fizzle out, causing you to defer your plans.

*The idea of having goals is to enjoy moving towards them.*

A well-formed goal is one that has all the elements to get you excited about it. The idea of meeting your goal fills you with desire, the best fuel to keep you motivated, especially when the going gets tough. In the section, **The Reason Behind Your Goal**, we saw that having a strong, personal reason behind your goal keeps you motivated.

If your goal is massive, it might prevent you from acting on it. Chunk it down to easy, actionable, intermediate goals to make it compelling.

## Self-reflection:

1. Does your goal pull you towards it?
2. Have you broken your goal down into actionable chunks?

## Ecology Check

Your health, along with the relationships you share with the people in your environment collectively forms your ecology. While defining your goal, you need to consider how its materialization will impact your ecology. For instance, if a person decides to shift to a new country to pursue her financial goals, she also needs to think about how she will raise her children in the new scenario. Or if you have an aggressive goal—like trying to reduce to half your weight in a month—you need to consider the impact of such a goal on your health.

If you miss the ecology check, you might face problems during execution, causing you to lose time and energy in backpedaling and redefining the goal.

John was one of the most competent business managers in his organization. His performance was excellent, however, his health was suffering. He was constantly tired because of his responsibilities at work. He had the skills but lacked the energy to do his job well.

John decided to exercise and eat healthy to regain his lost stamina. He enrolled in a gym near his house and scheduled his evenings for his workout sessions. He chalked out a new meal plan and handed it to his wife, Nancy, so she could prepare food for him.

After a few months of following this plan, can you guess what happened? John built his stamina like he wanted to. Nancy, on the other hand, resented his long hours away from home, be it at the office or at the gym. The extra work she had to put in to cook special meals for her health-conscious husband frustrated her. On days when she could not do so, John would be angry with her.

To become fit, John was ready to give up his evenings and his delicious, unhealthy food. What he did not realize was that along with these things, he was giving up something as important to him as his health—his relationship with his wife.

Eventually, John was physically fit but mentally unhappy. This did not feel like success to him.

*The ecology might not adapt to the goal. The goal needs to account for the ecology.*

### Self-reflection:

1. Does your goal fit into your whole system—your health, relationships, finances, and values?
2. If you met your goal, how will it impact you and your environment?
3. What will happen if you do not meet your goal?

Let's answer the above questions using John's case:

1. John's fitness goal helps him improve his

stamina. It also impacts his ecology as it increases his wife's responsibilities and reduces their time together.

2.  If John meets his goal, he will be able to carry out his duties better at work. It will impact his wife as she will have more to cook and less time with him.

3.  If he does not meet his goal, he might not be able to handle the work stress for much longer.

## Self-initiated and Self-maintained

*A goal has the greatest chance of materializing if it does not depend on other people or situations outside your control.*

Let's say, you are working for a certain company and your goal is to become the CEO by a certain date. The goal is well-defined but is not in your control because you will not appoint yourself as the CEO. You can have a goal of preparing for the position by building your skills. That way, when the time comes, you will be the ideal candidate. Competency building is in your control, hence making it a realistic goal to chase.

It's best to have a goal that you can commence on your own, one that doesn't rely on other people to begin or sustain. In John's case, we saw that when Nancy could not cook as per his diet, he would get angry with her. This is an example of a goal that is neither self-initiated nor self-maintained. John can take control back by not depending on Nancy. If he can arrange for the meals himself, it will smoothen out the process of achieving his fitness goal.

I sometimes meet people who tell me that they don't feel motivated to go on a morning walk. To solve this problem, they designate a person to wake them up in the morning and accompany them on the walk. While this is a good way to ensure that the walk happens, excessive dependency on the *walk buddy* might not work out in the long run.

<u>**Self-reflection:**</u>

1. Can you initiate and maintain your goal yourself?
2. Does achieving your goal require the contribution of people or circumstances outside your control? If so, can you redefine your goal?

## State the Context of the Goal

Imagine you are getting ready for a party and you ask two of your friends how you look. Your friend, a doctor, says that you look anemic and the other friend, a gym instructor, says that you look nice but need to work on your arms. Neither of the two could see you without the lens they wear.

If you do not define the context of your goal, you might unintentionally get into unrelated situations and continue to play out the goal-oriented behavior. A person who wants to become a sought-after lawyer needs to know the court in which she plans to excel. Acting as a lawyer around her family members might not fit well with her outcomes. Likewise, a boxer has goals in the context of a boxing ring, a manager manages her team at the workplace, and a teacher teaches her students at school. This is the context in which they operate.

Professionally, I work as a coach, conducting sessions with my clients in which I process their thoughts. However, if I coach people in my friends circle, they might perceive it as unsolicited advice. It is important for me to state the context of my goal while defining it, "I want to work as a coach with my clients in my coaching and training sessions."

**Self-reflection:**

1. When, where, and with whom are you going to achieve your goal? Define the context of your goal.

**State the Resources Required**

Irrespective of the goal, you will require certain resources to generate results. We can broadly divide these into two types:

**Internal resources** which include your beliefs and states of mind like courage, calmness, or determination that help you achieve your goals.

**External resources** which include time, money, people, books, workspace, etc. You might need a mentor to guide you, or money to start a new business. Time is a precious, limited resource that you can optimize by prioritizing your work.

Internal resources can help you create external resources. We will discuss this in greater detail in the upcoming section, Frames of Thinking.

## Self-reflection:

1.  What internal and external resources do you have to achieve your goal?
2.  What other resources do you need? What can you do right away to arrange for them?

**Exercise**

**Create a Hierarchy of your Goals**

1. Write three important goals for the upcoming week, month, and year. Also, write where you would like to be 5 years and 10 years from now.

2. Categorize your short-term and long-term goals on priority basis to gain clarity on what you need to focus on at the moment.

3. Pick one short-term goal and answer the questions provided in each section of Well-Defined Outcomes.

If you can find a person who is also interested in doing this exercise, it will be beneficial. Both of you can write your answers individually and discuss them with each other later.

At the end of this exercise, check if your goal is well-formed. If not, work towards finding the missing pieces.

When I conduct training programs, I have noticed that, at times, participants try to do this exercise by answering the questions verbally rather than writing them down. I insist they write their answers before discussing them, because:

1.  We tend to miss the finer details while speaking about our goals.
2.  There is no record of the definition of our goal if we were to state it verbally. Hence, we have nothing to refer to if we ever need clarity on what we set out to do.
3.  Writing imbibes the goal into our unconscious mind as it involves the body. This programs us to act on our goals and increases the chances of being successful at them.

6

# FRAMES OF THINKING

Have you noticed that sometimes two people who have the same goal and similar circumstances end up with diametrically different results? If their external resources are the same, the only plausible explanation for this is their frame of thinking.

❦

Peter and Jim were colleagues in an advertising agency. Both dreamt of launching their own company someday, but they lacked the skills. To build their competency, they needed to undergo training, however, the training programs were too expensive for them.

They were unhappy with their current job but didn't want to quit because of the security it provided them. They would often get together after work and discuss their aspirations. Jim found the idea of leaving a secure job to start his own enterprise too overwhelming and dropped it. Peter had many questions as well. He wondered:

"Will I have the money to train myself?"

"If I arrange for the money, will I have time to attend the training?"

"How will I manage my livelihood till my company turns profitable?"

One of Peter's core strengths was relentlessness. When he decided on a goal, he did everything in his power to solve the problems that stood in his way. He started looking up training institutes that provided the best programs. He found one that accepted the annual training fee in installments and joined the evening batch so he could attend his classes without missing out on his day job. He successfully completed the training program in a year's time.

Free to dedicate his evening hours towards his dream project, he got together with a few others he had met during the training and floated a company that provided advertising solutions. In a matter of time, Peter earned enough money from his enterprise to leave his day job. He hired a few people and trained them, so they could take over some of his responsibilities. As his team grew, his company also prospered.

One day Jim paid Peter a visit. It surprised him to see Peter's phenomenal growth in just a few years. He wondered what the secret behind his success was.

What do you think set Peter and Jim apart? They both lacked external resources such as time and money. However, Peter had internal resources that helped him create the required external resources. He created time for training by utilizing his evenings and managed his money by paying for the program in installments. He focused on the outcome, chalked out a plan, did not give up, and eventually succeeded. Besides hard work and a strategic plan, he had a frame of mind that helped him get there.

When we have a certain outcome in mind, it is necessary to provide a frame to our thinking. Otherwise, our thinking can go all over the place. We can jump from one topic to another and waste hours in futile thinking. It's like running on the spot—tiring and unproductive.

The frame of thinking that focusses on solutions and the resources you have is known as an **Outcome Frame.**

The frame of thinking that focusses on problems and the resources you don't have is known as a **Blame Frame.**

In any endeavor, your frame of thinking will largely decide the result. The more you think about problems, the more problems you will have. The more you think about solutions, the more solutions you will have. Both are there. It depends on what you are tapping into.

**Blame Frame**

Blame frame gets into the *why* of a problem, which results in storytelling. It can give you the cause of the cause of the cause, which isn't helpful. Let's say you are the manager of a team and your subordinate is routinely late to work. If you ask her, "Why are you late?" you hear the reason behind the delay—burnt breakfast, traffic jam, or parking issues. Despite the merit in these reasons, it does not help you meet your outcome of wanting her to arrive on time.

When you have an outcome in mind, you will get better results by exploring the *what* and *how* of things. Hence, a better question here will be, "What has to happen for you to come on time?" This will make her think on lines of your outcome. (A well-crafted question brings best results when conveyed respectfully. This gets communicated to the recipient through body language and tonality.)

It does not matter whether the question we ask ourselves is intelligent or not. Our unconscious mind will faithfully try to answer it. Have you noticed how little children rarely admit that they don't know something? That's exactly how our unconscious mind is. If we ask ourselves, "Why me?" it actively tries to answer the question. It might say-

"Because you are not smart enough."

"Because you didn't have the resources."

"Because of your tough childhood."

These thoughts leave us feeling helpless. We blame, judge, and complain. When someone else is to blame, we feel angry. When we are to blame, we feel guilty. Neither of these two states helps us move towards our goals.

The blame frame makes us pass the responsibility of our lives onto other people or situations. It makes us feel like we aren't capable of pulling ourselves out of issues. These issues get magnified as well. Eventually, we lose hope. This state of mind takes us further away from what we could have potentially achieved.

## Outcome Frame

In an outcome frame, people cut through everything that might have led to the problem and focus on what they can do in the moment to resolve it. It does not matter if these problems result from poor decisions or unfavorable circumstances, because of oneself or other people. The question is—what now?

*The point of power always lies in the present moment.*

If I notice a client has spent sufficient time in the blame frame, I usually flip it around to an outcome frame with a simple question, "What do you want in this situation?" This is followed by a few minutes of silence as the person stops in her tracks. The change of frame can disorient the person momentarily but has significant benefits soon after.

The blame frame creeps into our thinking, more so when we feel overwhelmed with problems. Awareness can help us switch to an outcome frame. Initially, this might require a conscious effort on our part. Once we have practiced it long enough, we will naturally gravitate towards an outcome frame.

When we are angry with people and complain about them, we are in a blame frame. When we stop complaining and ask them for what we need, we are in an outcome frame. This way, on changing the frame, we stand a better chance of getting what we want.

**Structure over Content**

In my coaching sessions, I rarely focus on *why* a person is having a certain problem. The question is—what is she doing to create her problem states, and how is she maintaining it? Once she faces an issue, does she drop it immediately or does she ruminate over it? Does she distract herself from her problems, or does she actively look for solutions?

If I need to feel exactly the way she is feeling, what do I have to do inside my mind? Once I understand her mental strategy, it becomes easy to facilitate solutions to her other problems as well because people tend to repeat their strategies.

*How you do anything is how you do everything.*

Instead of the content of the problem, it helps to focus on the structure of the thinking. Eliciting the structure is useful as it is the piece of the puzzle which puts everything in place. The problem could change frequently, but the structure of handling it usually remains the same.

Why do I have this problem? (Blame Frame) Gives you the problem that lies in the content.

How can I fix it? (Outcome Frame) Gives you the solution that lies in the structure.

For instance, an anxious person who plays worst-case scenarios, does it repeatedly without realizing that it is her mental movie that is causing the anxiety and not the situation. Asking her what is making her anxious doesn't help. The reason can change every day, but the strategy remains the same. What we want to know is, "What does she have to do inside her mind to feel differently?"

## Exercise

Think of a problem you are facing right now or an area where you want better results. Answer the following questions. Observe how you feel while answering them:

## Question Set 1

- "What's wrong?"
- "Why do I have this problem?"
- "How long have I had this problem?"
- "How does it limit me?"
- "What does this problem stop me from doing?"
- "Whose fault is it I have this problem?"
- "When was the last time I experienced this?"

Walk around and take a few deep breaths. Shrug off the feeling. Think about your favorite pastime.

Now bring the situation you just processed back to the screen of your mind. Note how you feel as you answer the following questions:

## Question Set 2

- "What do I want?"
- "By when do I want it?"
- "How will I know that I have it?"
- "When I get what I want, what else will improve in my life?"

- "What resources—external or internal—do I have available to help me with this?"
- "How can I best use the resources I have?"
- "What am I going to do now to get what I want?"

As you might have guessed already, Set 1 puts you in a Blame frame and Set 2 puts you in an Outcome frame. Check with yourself:

- How did you feel while answering questions from Set 1?
- How did you feel while answering questions from Set 2?
- What is clear to you after changing the frame of thinking?
- What actions can you take right away?

You can practice this exercise anytime you are stuck with a problem or want to improve on your results. Even if you don't have a breakthrough, the questions will keep your mind occupied in the right direction.

I have conducted this exercise with at least a few hundred people in my training programs and found strikingly similar results with each run. Answering Set 1 makes people feel dismayed, inadequate, and inept at solving their problems, whereas Set 2 makes them feel more in control of their situations. When I asked them to examine their feelings at the end of the exercise, they could observe what a change of frame could do for them. (I don't ask them for the content of their situation. The objective of this exercise is to understand the structure of their thinking, not the content.)

# LOGICAL LEVELS

Logical Levels is a model that describes six frames of reference that can alter human experiences. It is sometimes referred to as 'Levels of Change'. It serves as a great tool for when you need clarity on formulating your goals. If you ever find yourself saying, "I am not sure about what I want," you can use Logical Levels to understand your objective better.

This framework also helps if you are feeling stuck in a situation and are looking for a way forward, indicating at which level you require change. Understanding the interplay between the levels can help you design solutions that are in line with your overall mission.

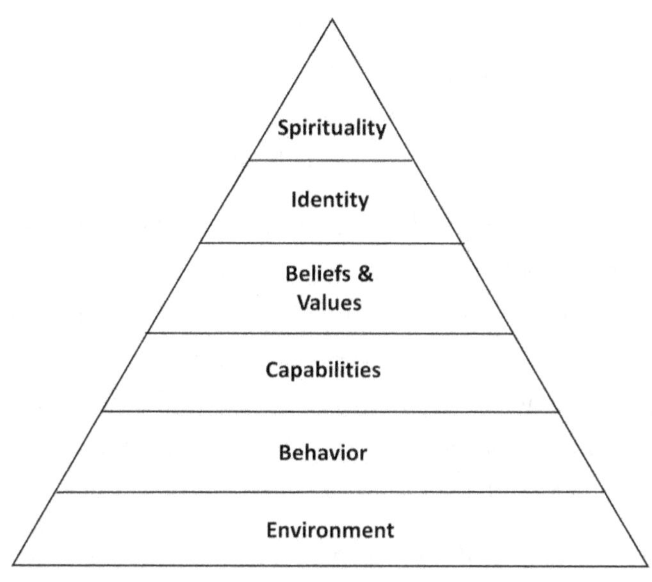

Logical Levels

## Environment

Think about a goal you achieved successfully. What were the contributing factors in your environment that helped you do so? Maybe there were people who mentored you, recommended your business to clients, or invested money in your venture. It could be an encouraging partner, personal or professional, who took care of your responsibilities while you pursued your goals. You will find these factors because your environment directly impacts the success you will experience in achieving your goals.

If you are a business owner, your environment could be your market, competitors, and the framework in which you run your business. If you are a manager at an organization, your environment could include your colleagues, subordinates, seniors, and clients.

Your environment also includes the things you need, like machines, tools, and your work space. Let's say I want to read a book, but I don't have the books I want to read. There is no place in my house where I can settle down with a book in silence. Under these environmental conditions, what are the chances that I will eventually read a book?

*For generating results, the environment needs to be conducive.*

While your home is not a part of your work environment, it forms a part of your ecology and needs to be accounted for. Hence, if you depend on your partner or employees to take care of the home while you are away at work, that forms a part of your environment too. If the work front is not taken care of, it impacts the home front and vice versa because you don't operate in water-tight compartments. You are the same person moving between environments.

One way to enhance the chances of success is to surround yourself with people who have already achieved what you want to achieve. The vibrational influence of those people will rub off on you. Your belief about your goal materializing will increase multifold. For instance, it would help a person trying to stay fit to surround herself with other people who also care for their fitness. When she sees the surrounding people eating healthy, exercising regularly, and taking care of themselves, she will subconsciously start mirroring their patterns.

On the other hand, if a health-conscious person is surrounded by people who binge eat and are lazy, she might lose her motivation to be fit. Day one, she might look at them and think that she need not exercise for an hour, maybe half an hour is enough because the others are not even doing that much. Day two, she might think that even half an hour is too much, it's far more relaxing to just kick back with some junk food. There is nothing wrong with it since *everyone* is doing it. Her sample space becomes limited to the people around her and she gradually picks up their patterns.

*You vibe with your tribe!*

Besides people who have achieved what you want to, it helps to have people in your environment who believe in your success. This can be tricky. When I say this in my training programs, I am usually countered with a question such as, "What can I do if my family doesn't believe in my success?"

I understand that there are elements in our environment that are not in our control, like what our family members think about our goals or how much they believe in us. This impacts our state of mind, which affects our results. In such a case, we need to shift focus back to what is in our control, which is our own thoughts and feelings, instead of dwelling on what is not in our control, which is the thoughts and feelings of others.

The more we focus on what is in our control, the more of what is not starts to come under our control. We need to keep our energy and attention on what *we* can do to achieve our outcomes. As we progress, there is a good chance that others will come around as well. Doing more than that is futile and we will end up exhausted from fighting things outside our control. (For more information on this please read the section on *Circle of Influence* in my book, "**What Will People Think?**")

### Self-reflection:

1. To meet your goal, what kind of environment do you need? Describe all the elements as vividly as possible.
2. What are the three things in your environment that currently support you in meeting your goals?
3. If there was one thing in your environment that you could change, what would you change, and how will that help you?

## Behavior

To achieve a goal, your behavior needs to align with the result. For instance, a person seeking a promotion will need to demonstrate the behavior required at the next level. One way to understand the required behavior is by observing a person who is already working successfully at that position.

A person who wants to become a trainer will need to undergo and conduct training. A person who wants to become fit needs to behave in a way that enables her to become fit, such as eating healthy, exercising, and caring for herself.

The overall behavior defines a person's attitude, which reflects the underlying belief system. An attitude differs from a belief because it is backed by action.

*Just because you believe something is possible doesn't mean you will do anything about it.*

### Self-reflection:

1. How is your current behavior helping you achieve your goal?
2. How does your behavior fit into your environment?
3. What behavioral changes can help you achieve your goal better?

## Capability

If behavior is what you do, then capability is what you know how to do. You need certain skills to pursue your goal. For instance, a manager needs to have people management skills, and a trainer needs to have training skills.

Some people have a natural talent for a job. You might have seen a teacher who, you felt, was born to teach. It serves as a bonus when what you want is in line with your inherent capabilities. You are likely to see this in people who are passionate about their work and successful at it.

If the capability does not exist at the level that is required, it can be developed through training. Organizations usually have a department for this, which enhances the skills people need as per their role. The act of developing capabilities is a desired behavior. The best training programs may be available, but if people don't enroll in them, it will not benefit them.

*Based on their behavior, people who are capable get better results.*

### Self-reflection:

1. What skills do you currently have that support you in achieving excellent results?
2. What other skills do you need to develop in

order to do better with respect to your goals?

3. What is the first step you can take towards enhancing your capability? Can you do it right away?

**Values and Beliefs**

Our values are personal and important to us. They help us know when something is right for us in our worlds. They follow a certain hierarchy—unique to each individual—by which some values are more important than others. If our core values are violated, we undergo emotional pain, because we live our values at an unconscious level.

Imagine a person who has *honesty* as her core value. She joins a job that requires her to take a bribe or lie regarding certain information to her clients. There might be some people who will not mind giving out small amounts of misinformation if it can save them money. However, a person who deeply values honesty will suffer at an emotional level daily. Instead of trying to change her values, it might be helpful for her to find a different job.

Your values are visible in your day-to-day actions. If you help people despite being busy, then caring is one of your values. If you speak the truth, even if it could get you into trouble, then honesty is one of your values. Observing yourself and the reasons for your actions can help you understand what your values are.

For you to be happy, it is important to have a goal that is aligned with your deeply held values. Otherwise, it will not bring you the intended happiness.

Values can be *moving toward* or *moving away* from. If you are *moving towards* money, you might take more risks financially. If you are *moving away* from loss, you might be conservative. Understand your goal with respect to the underlying strategy. One person exercises to stay fit, another to avoid hearing unpleasant things about her appearance. One person earns money to enjoy life while another person earns to avoid the pangs of poverty.

While defining your goal, start with asking yourself what is most important to you—money, fame, freedom, or something else? Are you moving towards your value or away from it?

I would recommend going over your values, particularly if a situation in your environment has hurt you and is hindering your progress. Use the Logical Levels model to check for any value misalignment.

(A list of commonly held values is available in the **'Being Yourself Journal'**. Download your free copy at romasharma.com. Please go over the list to identify your values.)

Similar to our values, our beliefs also operate at an unconscious level and constantly filter the incoming information. Our behavior results from our values and beliefs, both of which give us a sense of what is *right* and *wrong* for us. Both are deeply ingrained in our unconscious minds during our childhood years. However, there are certain differences between them. Beliefs are easier to change than values. Our beliefs change—sometimes randomly—over the course of our lives, whereas our core values rarely do. It's more painful if something violates our values rather than our beliefs. Anything that is in sync with our values feels good and anything that goes against hurts.

If there is a conflict between beliefs and values, we are likely to follow our values. For example, if you have a belief that talking to strangers is a bad idea, you might ignore an unknown person who approaches you. However, if that person is in trouble, you might help anyway, as *caring* is one of your core values. (As a coach, I find working on changing people's beliefs rather than their values to be more effective.)

If you are working as a part of a team, you can get significant results if your team members have values that match with yours and the organizations. Let's say you are hiring a person for a job. It helps to be clear about the values you are looking for in the candidate. I know of organizations that spend a lot of money training employees to be caring and humble. They experience little luck over time because they are expecting a shift in values which requires effort by the individuals. Others rooting for it cannot change it.

Hence, it is beneficial to screen peoples' values *before* hiring them for the job rather than taking them on and trying to change them later. One way to do this is to have a coach in the interview panel who focusses on value-elicitation.

## Self-reflection:

1.  What is important to you about your goal?
2.  What will achieving it get you?
3.  What are your core beliefs about your goal, yourself, and people in your environment?
4.  Do these beliefs support you in achieving your goal, or are they stopping you?

## Identity

What identity do you attach with yourself? If someone were to ask you, "Who are you?" what would you say? In my training programs, when I ask participants to introduce themselves, I hear responses such as-

"I am a coach."

"I am a manager."

"I am a schoolteacher."

I introduce myself as an author, coach, and trainer. It feels nice to identify as something that we like. However, it becomes an area of work when the profession becomes so much a part of a person's identity that the two are inseparable.

Anything that you identify with can become a source of attachment and pain. Let's say a person does her work sincerely. However, her manager points out that she needs to improve. If her work is an integral part of her identity, she will experience pain because of any perceived criticism of it.

Similarly, a lady whose definition of self is, "I am a mother," might associate the most with being a mother. If anything were to go wrong in her relationship with her child, she will suffer because it has hurt her identity.

When the result is not desirable, we can start with changing the way we refer to ourselves. We can disassociate by rephrasing the identity statements to what we *do* rather than who we *are*. The responses would be such as-

"I coach people."

"I manage people."

"I teach students at the school."

The statement, when structured like this, creates a distance between the profession and the identity of the person. Disidentification reduces the intensity of the problem and needs to be done only if required. For instance, if a person says that she will quit smoking but

also says, "I am a smoker," she will have difficulty quitting because smoking merges with her identity.

Other examples of unhelpful identity statements are, "I am fat", "I am an addict," or "I am depressed". A person is not a smoker or an addict. She demonstrates the behavior of smoking or being addicted to something. She is not depressed. She is creating thoughts that depress her, which is a behavior.

Separate the behavior from the identity for freedom from something undesirable. Include the behavior in the identity to gain something desirable. You can call yourself a jogger if it helps you stay fit.

*Create an identity for yourself that is in line with your goals.*

## Self-reflection:

1. Who are you?
2. How does your goal relate to your identity?
3. Does your goal agree with all parts of yourself?

## Spirituality

How do you relate to life and other people in this world? Represent it metaphorically. Are you the lotus that blooms in marshy lands, or are you the sunshine that spreads warmth equally on all?

To experience satisfaction on the successful materialization of your goal, it needs to be in harmony with your spiritual self. What is more important to you than yourself? What will you happily give yourself up for? This cause or idea, if unfulfilled, could leave you with a sense of emptiness even if you have achieved your goal. You might wonder if this is all there is to your goal. For instance, spiritually if you like to give to others but your goal requires you to only take, you will experience dissatisfaction.

Knowing that your work has made the world a better place can be very nourishing. Think about the impact you would like to leave on humanity—who will benefit from your work and how? This will take you beyond your immediate problems and connect you to your higher purpose.

## Self-reflection:

1. Does your goal align with your highest intent and purpose in life?
2. Is your goal a part of something bigger and more important than you?
3. How does your goal impact other people in the world? Does it improve their lives in any way?

## Integration of Levels

In the Logical Levels model, it is important to note that the level of difficulty in bringing about change gradually increases from the base of the pyramid (the environment level) to the tip (the spiritual level). A change at the lower levels might affect the higher levels. As you go higher up the pyramid, you get more leverage. Hence, a change at the higher levels will definitely impact the lower levels. These levels are different frames of human experience which work in tandem with each other. Let's look at some instances of how that happens. (To clearly indicate which level we are referring to, the level has been written in **bold**.)

When your **values** match the values of the people in your **environment**, it results in a collective **behavior** that is coherent. Such a group is likely to share a great rapport resulting in increased productivity. This makes it easier to achieve goals.

Whatever training you undergo to develop your skills and **capabilities** will not be useful unless you align your goal with your **identity** and **spiritual** purpose.

Let's say, you have the **capability** of achieving your goal and your **behavior** reflects that as well. Luckily, you also have a great work **environment** that has people whose **behavior** and **capability** matches yours. However, if your **beliefs** about these people are not helpful, it will impact the overall results you achieve. If your **beliefs** are helpful but your goal clashes with your **identity** and with that of others in your **environment,** it will be hard to materialize such a goal.

This is how the different logical levels interplay to create our results.

Sam is an employee of an organization, who has been working hard for a promotion for a few years. Unfortunately, he is not happy with his team. He believes his manager is controlling and his teammates shift their workload onto him. A few months later, his resentment reaches a point where he decides to quit.

Sam speaks to Anthony, who works for the human resource department. Anthony asks Sam to change his team instead of quitting his job. He thinks it will help Sam keep his rating in the organization and get promoted in the next cycle.

Sam implements the suggestion. Things are better for a few months. Over time, he notices similar problems to the ones he was facing in his previous team. He finds his manager to be overbearing and feels that his teammates are taking advantage of him by making him do most of the work. Once again, he wants to quit. He speaks to Anthony about his issues.

Anthony tells Sam that moving out of the organization could present bigger challenges like finding a new job, developing new skills, and adjusting to the culture. Sam already has the capabilities for the current job. If he could just move to a different team instead of quitting, it might help him.

Due to constantly changing teams, Sam could not get the promotion. He didn't stay long enough in one team to prove his worthiness, despite being capable. Eventually, Sam felt frustrated and considered himself a loser. This demotivated him further.

At which logical level do you think Sam needs resolution? Let's examine his situation.

Sam is having difficulty in his environment. He has beliefs like that his manager is controlling and his teammates take advantage of him. Despite being capable, he could not succeed because of his negative beliefs about others.

The change of environment did not help because he carried the same beliefs to the new environment and replayed the pattern. Hence, although it appears like the problem was at an environment level, it was actually at a belief level. If Sam believes that the way he has been behaving is the only right way, it again points to work required at the belief level.

Sam's capability level might need some evaluation as well. Having only the technical capabilities required for the role was insufficient. He also needs to develop interpersonal and conflict management skills to meet his outcomes. If he has a manager whom he finds controlling, or team members who, he believes, shift their workload onto him, he needs to develop the communication skills to express his views to them. This will set the expectations right and prevent him from repeatedly trying to escape difficult situations.

Sam needs to understand his spiritual self as well. How does he connect to the rest of the world? What is more important to him than himself? All levels need examination.

Eventually, when Sam is unable to meet his goal of getting a promotion, he feels frustrated and believes that he is a *loser*. This is an identity level statement. Once he labels himself that way, he will create more negative beliefs about himself, which—if held over time—can further reduce his chance of getting promoted.

In a coaching session, if I come across clients making such identity level statements, I change the level at which the person is operating. From identity, I take them to the level of beliefs or capability. For instance, "I am a loser," can be shifted to "What specific capabilities do you need to develop to do this job well?" (Notice that not only has the logical level changed, but the blame frame has also been converted to an outcome frame.)

If my client mentions an issue in the environment such as, "People just don't co-operate with me," I scan for underlying beliefs by asking questions such as, "What are some of your beliefs about the people you work with?" Here, I have moved the level of introspection from environment to belief.

*Even if the presenting problem seems to operate at one level, you might need to scan other levels, till you find the appropriate one to work on.*

## Exercise

Draw a line on the ground. Take a set of six cards, one for each logical level of change. Label each card with the name of the level on it. Place the cards along the line in the right sequence (refer: Logical Levels diagram). Write the self-reflection questions on a piece of paper. These questions are present at the end of each level in the description of Logical Levels.

Stand at Level 1 (environment) and answer the self-reflection questions for Level 1. Now take a step forward and enter Level 2 (behavior). Answer the self-reflection questions for Level 2.

Move forward gradually from one level to another, answering the questions pertaining to every level. Continue walking this way till you reach the tip of the pyramid. When you get there, turn around and walk back one level at a time again, introspecting with the reflective questions at each level, this time with the new awareness you have gained by doing the exercise.

**Please note:**

1. You can do this exercise yourself, although it is better to do it with a coach. That way you will have a person to take care of the procedure while you focus on your internal process.
2. Instead of drawing a line and writing the levels on the ground, you can walk along an imaginary line. This works as long as you can remember the levels and reflect on the associated questions suitably.

Once you have completed the exercise immediately make a note of what you gathered from it:

1. What are your strengths? What are you already doing well?
2. What are your areas of improvement? Where do you need a change?
3. What resources—internal or external—do you need to create that change?
4. List down the actions you can take to bring about that change. Can you start now?

You might stumble upon some fantastic ideas during this exercise. Encapsulate them into actionable items and fix timelines by when you can implement them. The more information you have regarding the change you want, the higher is the chance that you will achieve it. The best way to get a return for the effort spent in doing this exercise is to act on your new learning *immediately*.

8

# THE INTERNAL THINKING ENGINE

In the section Your Two Minds, we saw how thoughts create feelings and feelings create behavior. Since behavior generates the actions that make you successful, let us understand: (1) how a behavior gets generated and (2) what can be done to change it, if required.

Here is the definition of some terms used in the description:

**Feeling state**: is the same as a **feeling**. It is also referred to as a **state**.

**Resourceful state**: is a state in which you are feeling good and are likely to generate significant results. This state is different for each individual. Examples of some resourceful states are happy, confident, calm, etc.

**Unresourceful state**: is a state in which you are not your best and might find it difficult to generate desired results. This state is unique to each individual, such as disappointed, depressed, angry, or frustrated.

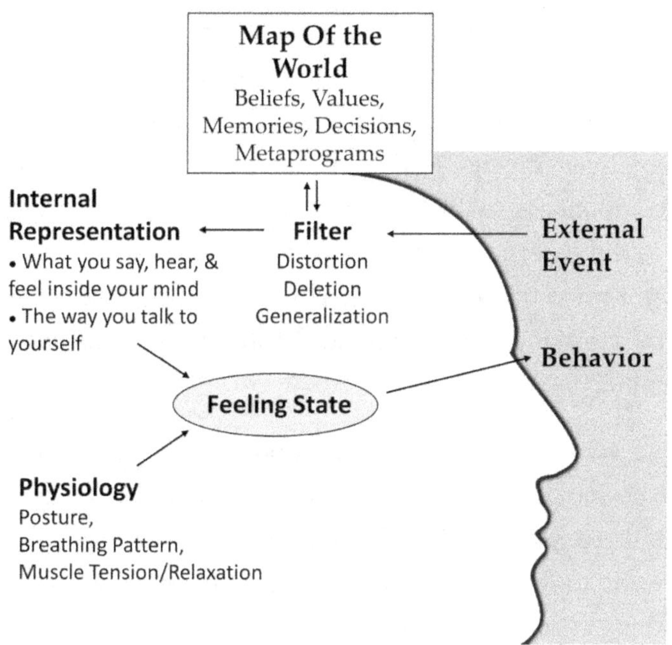



**The Internal Thinking Engine**

An external event has a visual, auditory, and kinesthetic component (what you see, hear, and feel outside in the world). When you internalize the event, it gets recreated inside your mind as a movie which also has a visual, auditory, and kinesthetic component (what you see, hear, and feel inside your mind). For instance, right now you can hear some sounds in your environment. You can see this book as well as feel the temperature of the air on your skin. This information is external to you. Now close your eyes and go back to a time when you were on a vacation. What do you see, hear, and feel?

Personally, I went to a beach, saw the blue ocean, heard the water splashing against the rocks, and felt the sand beneath my feet. The air was warm and humid. This is my inner movie—with visual, auditory, and kinesthetic components—which creates my internal representation of the external event. Right now, I am not on a beach and none of this is happening. Yet, I can experience it by accessing the information stored in my unconscious mind.

As you remember your vacation, notice how you feel. The movie you play inside your mind and the way you talk to yourself largely decides your feelings. If you want to feel good, play more positive movies, such as things you are grateful for or enjoy.

## The Filtering Mechanism

Is our internal representation identical to the external event? When you recalled your last vacation, was it *exactly* the way it happened? Probably not. We all have specific, unique ways of filtering an incoming stream of information and interpreting it. That is why two witnesses of the same event report it differently. It's not that one of them is incorrect. It's just that they created two different versions based on their unique filtering of an identical event. One might remember what she heard while another might remember what she saw or felt.

Broadly, there are three types of filters at work in our unconscious mind. (These are high-level blanket filters. Besides these, there are countless filters that run at an unconscious level.)

## Distortion

Has it happened that you saw someone from a distance and thought it was your friend, but when you took a closer look it was someone else? This is an example of visual information being distorted.

Similar distortions happen at a cognitive level when we interpret information in a way that does not match with the external reality. For instance, someone refuses to do you a favor and you believe the person doesn't like you. This may not be true; the person could have other reasons for not being able to help you. However, the distortion could create an emotional response in you. You might not have any reason to back your belief, but the feeling is real.

## Deletion

If you are in a crowded room and someone says your name, you cancel out all the noise in the room and pay attention to them. It is possible that you were just being referred to. Yet, it draws all your attention. Does that mean that the rest of the sounds in the room suddenly ceased to exist, or were they muted out only for you?

The sounds were there, but you deleted them by withdrawing attention from them. You might have noticed that, at times, your friend and you recall a certain incident differently. You have unconsciously deleted some information that your friend could recall, and vice versa.

**Generalization**

The brain learns through generalization. You know that on a switch, down is on and up is off. You know that a green traffic light means go and red means stop. Similarly, you might have learned to use a keyboard or drive a car, but now you can use any. Generalization makes life simple. It saves time and energy. If we had to learn everything repeatedly, it would drain us out.

Generalization happens in thinking as well. How would you respond if someone said that all cats are white? You might believe that this person has a limited sample space of cats and is using that to draw conclusions about *all* cats.

Sometimes we extend an experience in one context to all other contexts, like there is no exception to our experience. For instance, a person who suffered at the hands of an authoritative caregiver in their childhood could write off *all* authoritative people as bad. Such generalizations might need re-examination, especially if they negatively impact the person.

## Changing the Filtering Process

At the end of a training program, I don't remember every detail of each participant. I might not be able to recall how many people were wearing glasses or jackets. This information was available to me when I was conducting the program, but I unconsciously deleted it as it was not important to me.

In larger groups, I rarely remember the name of each participant, and refer to them by their company name. This is an example of deletion of information along with generalization. If I create beliefs about the group, it could very well be my distortion.

We can't stop filtering. Even if we understand the concept perfectly, it is going to continue unconsciously, because we are being bombarded every second by millions of bits of information which are impossible for the human mind to process. Hence, we pay selective attention to some information and delete, distort, and generalize the rest.

*Our filtering mechanism decides what we pay attention to.*

Since we can't stop filtering, what works is to have a method of filtering that puts us into a resourceful state. What if we deleted information related to feeling less than positive about ourselves? We can create distortions (or beliefs) that put us into great states. Instead of having a negative distortion like, "People don't like me," I can have a positive distortion like, "People like me. I am lovable." There will be people who don't like me but distorting in that direction puts me in an unresourceful state.

A generalization that is great to have is, "Every problem has a solution." It gives us tremendous freedom to look for solutions and be successful.

When I say this to my clients, I usually get the question, "Our map of the world and filtering works at an unconscious level. Can I consciously delete, distort, and generalize information like this?" My response is-

Our unconscious program runs automatically. To create a new pattern requires work. While you might not change the filtering mechanism by telling yourself to delete the events when someone hurt you or to dissolve unhelpful generalizations, it is possible to make those changes incrementally through self-work—regularly reading good quality material, journaling, meditating, undergoing training, coaching, etc.

*Anything you do consciously, you have not yet mastered. Repetition can make a thought pattern a part of your unconscious process.*

If you can catch the unhelpful distortion/deletion/generalization and filter information in a way that helps you, over time, this will become your new unconscious process. It is important to check your thoughts because your thoughts become your behavior, your behavior becomes your habits and your habits become your destiny.

## How to Change Your Feelings

Your feelings depend on what you focus on at any point of time and what meaning you give your object of focus. By changing either of the two, you can change your feelings.

When a child is hurt, her mother talks about the moon and fairies while nursing her wound. This changes the child's focus, making her feel better. You might have also heard a child being told things like, "Bearing this pain will make you tough." This is an interpretation given to help her feel better.

While we may or may not want to distract ourselves to change our feelings, it helps to focus on thoughts that make us feel good, like what we are grateful for or the amazing future experiences that await us. It also helps to interpret situations in a way that supports our happiness.

Where is your attention focused? + What is your interpretation? Results in your feeling.

You might have seen two siblings whose childhood experience differs widely. One remembers their childhood as intolerable, and the other says that it was wonderful. Was their childhood wonderful or intolerable? Turns out, they both are right based on how they represented their situation to themselves. It is possible that one child experienced childhood differently than the other due to external factors. Let's say, the parents were kinder to one of them for some reason. Even so, the internal representation will trump the external factors and create a helpful or unhelpful experience.

When people are hurt by someone else's actions or words, a common advice given to them is, "Ignore it." It stems from the belief that once we learn the art of ignoring others, we can be peaceful inside. There is some merit in that thought. However, we can't just *ignore* something that hurts us because we are not punching bags. We are human beings with actual feelings.

People who appear to be good at ignoring situations might not be letting go of their hurt internally. The ones who can have most likely interpreted the situation in a way that helps them feel better. For instance, they might believe that the people who hurt them were themselves under stress. This interpretation helps them move ahead peacefully.

This does not mean that one should create imaginary positive interpretations or become delusional in order to overcome problems. It just means that once you have chosen a positive interpretation and put yourself into a resourceful state, it will be easier to solve the problem at hand.


**Your Map of the World**

Your map of the world comprises of your beliefs, memories, decisions, metaprograms, attitudes, values, and other factors related to your life experiences. Your metaprogram is an internal unconscious program that decides what part of the incoming information to pay attention to. All these factors are unique to an individual, making the map unique as well. Your map is like the GPS you unconsciously refer to while navigating through the world.

The map is not the territory, which means there is no *one reality*. Since each one of us filters and interprets information differently, we all have our own versions of reality. Whichever way we choose to represent things to ourselves becomes our reality. This representation could be marginally or starkly different from the way things are.

The map is not the territory, but if it resembles the structure of the territory, that accounts for its usefulness. If your internal representation closely matches the external situations, it will help you navigate through them smoothly.

We saw in the section on Logical Levels how our beliefs affect our results. Imagine having beliefs like, "People take advantage of me if I let my guard down." Would it help us get the intended result in our environment? Perhaps it might, but it will require more effort. People will sense our lack of trust and respond accordingly. It could be a lot easier to achieve the same result if we had useful beliefs like, "People are trustworthy and nice to me," (and deal with the ones that do not fit into this belief). A change in belief alters our map and gets us better results.

It helps to have a map that represents the outside world in a way that consistently gets us the results we are looking for. With an improperly structured map, we have to struggle more. It will be like navigating through Mexico with a map of Alaska. To navigate easily, we need to use a map of Mexico that closely resembles its territory.

Having principles that consider what is good for others, and help us meet our outcomes, is one way to have a properly structured map. Decision-making becomes easy and chances of success increase. Changing frequently based on what is convenient or beneficial for oneself might help meet immediate goals but might not work out in the long run.

We also need to ensure that our map is up to date. If we hold on to a map that was created in childhood and use it to navigate situations in adulthood, it will be as ineffective as trying to navigate a city with a decades-old map. Things have changed. New buildings have come up. Old structures have been demolished. It's time to update the map. Based on observation, refine your map till it helps you easily achieve your outcomes.

In a coaching session, I spend time understanding the client's map of the world. What are her core beliefs, values, and the unconscious decisions she has made (maybe in childhood)? What is most important to her? How does she represent the world internally?

Once I create her map, it will be easy for me to see where her experiences are coming from and what we can change to get better results. This requires me to first leave my map of the world outside the session, to avoid directing her based on what *I* think is right rather than what might work for her. Counselors and coaches need to be alert for such slippages as they creep in on us, despite our best intentions.

**To summarize:**

1.  We create our internal representation using our visual, auditory, and kinesthetic senses. These —along with the way we talk to ourselves— form the building blocks of our inner experience.
2.  Each one of us has a unique map based on which we filter incoming information and create internal representations of external events, causing us to live in an interpreted reality.
3.  Our internal representations are not identical to the external events. However, if they closely resemble each other, it is helpful to us.

## The Mind and Body Connect

We saw in the section on Your Two Minds that there are certain feeling states that support people in moving towards their goals. For instance, while training I need to be calm, confident, and focused to generate an optimum result. I can train when I am stressed, but the result might not be satisfactory.

Besides internal representation, your feeling states are created by your physiology, that is, your body. Depending on your breathing pattern, muscle tension/relaxation, and postures, your body generates feelings. The blood sugar level and the sleep you've got determines your willpower to carry out your tasks. Have you noticed that sometimes a person who is sick, hungry or tired looks irritable? This is because the mind and the body are a part of the same system. What impacts one, impacts the other. Let's do an exercise to understand this better.

**Exercise**

1. Go back to a time when you set a plan in action, executed it well, and nailed your goal. Do you remember how it felt? Stand the way you were standing and breathe the way you were breathing when that happened. Hold this posture for a few moments.

2. Notice how wonderful you feel as you recall that event.

3. Shake off the feeling. Think about your favorite food. Return to the exercise.

4. Recall a time when you set a plan in action, worked hard towards your goal, but it did not materialize. Stand the way you were standing when you found out that your effort did not bring you the intended result. Breathe the way you were breathing. In a few minutes, you will notice feeling disappointed. You might also experience other emotions such as anger or frustration based on how you felt back then.

5. Take a deep breath. Shake off the feeling. Think about your favorite movie. Return to the exercise.

6. Note down how you felt when you practiced the first posture versus the second. You might notice that the posture of your body and your breathing pattern changes the feeling you experience.

**Try this**: If, in the future, you are in an unresourceful state, assume the victory pose—hold your arms up in the air with your chin pointing up. Imagine being victorious at something and breathe that way. In a few minutes, you will experience a change of state.

## The Cybernetic Loop

We saw that your physiology and your internal representation impacts your feeling states. Both these factors work together like a cybernetic loop. They feed each other to create feelings.

How you feel physically impacts your state of mind. When you are feeling fit, you tend to internally represent the world as a great place to be. When you are feeling physically tired or unwell, you are irritable. The world is no longer a fun place. The world did not alter, but your physical fitness created a different representation for you.

Let's look at the other way around—how your internal representation impacts your physiology. When the way you represent things to yourself makes you feel good, doesn't your body feel good as well? On the other hand, when the way you represent things to yourself makes you unhappy, have you noticed how heavy your body feels?

The effect of your internal representation of events is visible in your physiology, and vice versa. (As we saw in the previous section, the mind and the body are a part of the same system.)

*Whenever you need to change your feeling state, you can change your physiology or internal representation.*

You can change your internal representation by working on your map of the world. Changing the map tweaks the filtering mechanism and creates a new, more useful internal representation. (In my coaching sessions, I usually work on my client's beliefs as it gets me excellent results. We will go over ways to change beliefs later in the book.)

To change your feelings using your physiology, decide which activity creates a state change for you—yoga, breathing exercises, meditation, aerobics, dance, sports etc.—and use it to find a resourceful state. I don't mean to suggest that we dance our troubles away. We are doing these exercises to enter a resourceful state so we can deal with our problems better. Let's say, I am feeling disappointed. I might not be able to resolve the issue in that same state of mind. If I pause for a short while and do some breathing exercises, it might calm me down. I can then return to the problem in a better frame of mind to resolve it. You need to find the best ways that effect change for you.

To change your feeling state, it is best to work on both your physiology and your internal representation simultaneously. Otherwise, you might feel better in the body only to return to the old interpretations and re-create the previous feelings of anger, sadness, etc. For example, a person feeling stressed might meditate and feel better but return to feeling frustrated by repeating her old interpretation of the situation.

**The Key to Being Successful**

To achieve your goals, you need to-

Consistently represent information to yourself in a way that puts you in a resourceful state—one that empowers you to take the necessary actions towards your desired goals.

Write the above statement and put it up in a prominent place. It summarizes everything discussed so far on how to engineer success by using your internal thinking engine. Look at the statement frequently and say it aloud, to help it seep into your unconscious mind.

If you work hard and don't get what you want, read the above key statement, and create a powerful internal representation for yourself. Tweak your map by believing that you cannot *fail*. Even if you don't get the intended result, you still got feedback which will eventually lead to success.

Let's go back to the case of Sam we read about in the section on Integration of Levels and examine his thinking engine—filtering of information, map of the world, internal representation, feeling states, and the resultant behavior. Let's see what can bring him closer to his desired goal, which is the promotion.

Sam has beliefs about his manager being controlling and teammates taking advantage of him. These beliefs come from his map of the world. Based on this, he creates an internal representation of the way his colleagues are, by filtering information in his unique way. He might have deleted the times when his manager was not controlling or when his team members did their work themselves. He might have generalized one episode of work being passed onto him as people *always* doing so. What if the work assigned to him was apt for him? Thinking that his teammates were dumping irrelevant work onto him could be his distortion.

Post filtering, Sam's perception is created. His internal representation of the people in his environment becomes the interpreted reality in which he lives. This could manifest in his body as fatigue or pain. The combination of his internal representation and physiology will decide his feeling states, which we saw were frustration and demotivation. These are unresourceful states which disempower him from taking the necessary actions to move towards his goal.

If Sam were to undergo coaching, the process would start with eliciting information that was lost in filtering via distortion, deletion, and generalization. This can be done by asking questions around his experience. For example:

"How do you know that your manager is controlling?"

"What makes you believe that people are taking advantage of you?"

"How will changing teams or quitting the company help you?"

We don't mean to minimize Sam's experience. His manager might be controlling, and his team members might be taking advantage of him. However, the responsibility for change still needs to be brought back to Sam.

In a coaching session, when I hear the problems that people face, I bear in mind that they are only giving me their perspective. This is not necessarily the way things are. Unless I elicit information by asking effective questions, I cannot facilitate a solution that works well for the person.

*Recovering information that was lost in filtering makes the person's map richer, which, in turn, provides more choices to the*

Hence, by doing this exercise, Sam will get sufficient clarity about changing his situation. Once he works on his map of the world, starting with his beliefs, he will see a shift in his filtering process and therefore the representation of his environment. He might not think of his managers as overbearing or teammates as people who shift their work onto him. He is likely to feel better after interpreting things differently and consequently make better decisions. He might decide to communicate with his co-workers about what he needs instead of switching teams each time.

In a good frame of mind, we make excellent decisions and are usually in an outcome frame. In a disturbed frame of mind, we feel helpless and tend to enter a blame frame. The way we feel decides what results we will get. If we are not happy with the results, we need to examine our map of the world, change our filtering process, represent things differently to ourselves, and take action.

Sam's example was set in a professional environment. Let's see how we can achieve our personal goals by using the same process.

Tina and Michael are a couple who plan on taking a vacation in the upcoming holidays. Tina has cleared her work schedule and is ready to make the trip. Michael, however, is unable to do so. His project is pressed against a deadline and isn't going well. He is trying hard to finish as much work as possible on time. He has not mentioned his difficulties to Tina because he does not want her to stress over it.

Tina is waiting late every evening for Michael and is wondering what's keeping him. She imagines him to be partying with his friends and believes that he has not responded to their vacation plan because he does not care. She doesn't trust him to be working on it.

Finally, one evening, Tina decides to leave home. When Michael returns home from work, he finds her waiting for him with her bags packed. He wonders what the matter is. She tells him she is moving out for a while because she needs some space.

This confuses Michael, as he cannot understand the reason behind her leaving abruptly. He feels miserable as he worked so hard to take her on a vacation, and she isn't being understanding. He believes she doesn't love him.

Tina's map of the world has certain beliefs that might not be working for her. She believes that Michael is not trustworthy. When there is an external event—him coming home late—she creates an internal representation of him having fun, which makes her angry.

Tina might have deleted the times when Michael made time for her. She might have generalized his coming home late to extend to *always* rather than something that started recently. She distorted it to mean that he doesn't care. After filtering, her representation created a feeling of anger which translated into the behavior of leaving home. Hence, the goal of going on a vacation did not materialize.

Her beliefs can be challenged to retrieve information that was lost in filtering by asking questions such as-

Is there any reason to believe that Michael cannot be trusted?

Is he *always* late?

What has to happen for her to feel like she has been cared for?

Once lost information is recovered, she might represent things more accurately to herself. That will make her map of the world resemble the territory. To clarify, if she asks Michael about his side of the story, her internal representation will be better aligned with the external event. She is likely to be more compassionate when she realizes that Michael was working hard so he could take a vacation with her. That will increase their chances of going on a vacation, if not now, then in the future.

Let's examine Michael's filtering process. He deleted the fact that he did not communicate his work-related issues to Tina. Had he told her about his problems, Tina might have been empathetic. He assumed that if he told her, she would stress over it. This is a distortion. He believes he can read her mind. Finally, when she leaves the house, he creates another distortion that she did so because she doesn't love him. This interpretation results in him feeling miserable.

## What Decides Your Behavior?

We saw that feeling states lead to a person's behavior. However, in a certain state, is everybody's behavior identical? Probably not. If two people are equally angry because of the same reason, one might become verbally abusive while the other might sulk in despair. What decides how a person will behave?

One factor that decides a person's behavior is what her role models demonstrated when she was growing up. If Tina saw her mother as a person who did not trust anybody, this belief—*people are not trustworthy*—may have been ingrained in her mind unconsciously. She might be playing this belief out in adulthood without realizing it. If her mother expressed her anger by lashing out at others, Tina might do the same.

There are other factors that determine how a person could behave in a given feeling state. If a person's behavior in her childhood got her the intended response from others, it might become her routine behavior in adulthood as well. For instance, if Tina, as a child, got what she wanted by sulking, then unconsciously she might decide that sulking is a good strategy, and carry this into adulthood. This might not be the best way out but will continue to be exercised till she hits a roadblock and decides to change.

*Knowing the reason behind the type of behavior is not as important as addressing the feeling behind it.*

9

———

## SOURCE OF BELIEFS

There are many ways in which beliefs get formed over the course of a person's life. Let's go over some common sources of beliefs and what we can do to change them if needed.

## 1) Environment Fosters Beliefs

We saw in the section on Logical Levels that our environment impacts our beliefs. If we were raised in an environment of possibilities, we are more likely to have beliefs about things being achievable. However, if we were raised in an environment where people blamed others and took no responsibility, we might believe that we are helpless victims.

In a person's childhood, the early learning environment impacts the tender mind that is in the process of creating a world view. A little baby does not have any beliefs. She is creating them. Her mind is like soft clay, easily impressionable. This clay solidifies over time, making it resistant to change.

You might not have chosen the environment in which you were raised. However, as an adult, you can design an environment of your choice—one that increases the chances of success. Find at least five people who have achieved what you want and spend time with them. It will help foster positive beliefs. For instance, as a trainer, I can join a group of action-oriented trainers (even an online group will help). As I exchange notes with them, I will slowly start absorbing their beliefs. Things that I once thought were difficult might not seem so anymore.

We see similar effects when we read stories about people who succeeded in their outcomes. If I believe I do not have the resources to actualize my dream project and I read the story of a person who succeeded despite the lack of basic necessities, it could alter my beliefs. I might not be able to come up with an excuse for not working on my goals. Success stories have been motivating people since time immemorial. Reading them can be made a part of one's daily routine.

## 2) Past Experiences

The results we have created in the past impact our beliefs about our ability to create them in the future. Has it happened that you did not believe you could achieve a certain goal till you did it once, after which, your belief changed and you became better at it?

If you want to succeed at something, just do it once. You will believe that you can do it again. This belief will motivate you to act on your goals. I once met a student who could not clear her exams in a particular subject. She worked hard and scored well in that subject once. Going forward, her performance improved in other subjects as well.

Students perform well in an exam they believe they are prepared for, even if the exam questions are out-of-syllabus. If you tell someone, "Why bother studying all this? It will not be asked," it helps to remember that while questions might not be asked on that topic, it will certainly add to the belief of being well-prepared which will contribute to good results.

Our experiences create beliefs through emotions. When we experience an event associated with an emotional charge—whether positive or negative—we form a belief. For example, if I felt great because someone helped me, I might create a belief about that person being kind. However, if the same person refuses to help me, and that hurts me, I might create a new belief about that person being unkind.

*The greater the emotional charge associated with the event, the stronger is the resultant belief.*

To catch unhelpful beliefs from our past requires awareness and willingness on our part to change. Otherwise, the past will re-create itself in the future and we might find ourselves saying, "This *always* happens to me." We will go over this in greater detail in the section on Self-Fulfilling Prophecy.

### 3) Imagination Creates Beliefs

If you experience results in advance, you increase the likelihood of creating those results in the future. Visualize yourself, with complete conviction, as being successful in your endeavors. Your mind cannot distinguish between what you vividly imagine and what is. If you go about your life feeling great about having achieved your goal, you will draw situations to yourself that will help you get there. Live it and breathe it to achieve it.

Imagine you are part of a movie. The director asks you to rehearse the part of a charismatic and confident person. As per this role, you walk into a room and smile at everybody. When you talk, people look at you with amazement. They can't believe you exist!

As soon as your scene starts, you walk in and play your part. Your confident body language and speech amazes people. By the end of the scene, you seem to have blended into the character. You are feeling confident around people because you saw how they reacted to you. If you rehearse this scene repeatedly, that feeling will come naturally to you.

Let's look at another scene you have in the movie. In this scene, you are anxious. You are not confident enough to talk to anybody, and your anxiety level increases with every passing minute. Soon it becomes visible in your body language and people laugh at you.

After you rehearse this scene, notice how the anxiety appears in your body. Your heart pounds as it plays images of people making fun of you. If you rehearse this scene multiple times, you will feel that way even after the rehearsal ends.

Your imagination created your belief. In Scene 1, you imagined yourself to be confident and started believing it to a point of living it. In Scene 2, the same thing happened with believing that you are socially anxious. The more you get into character, the stronger is the effect.

Haven't we all created some unhelpful beliefs using our imagination? For instance, if a person doesn't smile at us, we could believe she doesn't like us—chances are she might have been preoccupied and didn't notice us.

Imagine yourself to be a person who can achieve *anything* you desire. Repeat it with emotional intensity till you completely believe in it. Your belief will manifest your goal.

# Exercise

| The Belief you want to change | What would you like to believe instead? | What will improve in your life because of this new belief? |
|---|---|---|
|  |  |  |
|  |  |  |

Belief Change Table

1. Draw a table like the one illustrated above. In the first column, write a belief you have which you would like to change. Example: "When people contradict me, I believe they don't like me."

2. In the second column, write what you would like in place of this belief. Example: "I would like to be comfortable with people contradicting me."

3. In the third column, write how your life would be better if you adopted this new belief. Would it help you have better relationships? Make more friends? Do better in your business?

4. Close your eyes and imagine vividly—with sensory-specific information—what will you see, hear and feel once you have made this change.

# 10

## SELF-FULFILLING PROPHECY: THOUGHTS ARE THINGS

You manifest things into your life with your unconscious thoughts. Whatever you thought about yesterday, you saw in your life today. Likewise, whatever you think about today will appear in your life tomorrow. Look around you. You might see walls, furniture, or lamps—things that someone thought about in the past. The person held onto the thought of creating it, and it appeared in the future. This happens because thoughts are things.

Let's say, you are a salesperson and you want to increase your income by selling better. Your product is priced at $100, but you do not believe it is worth that much. You try to convince your clients to buy it but somehow, they aren't interested. Wonder why? Your body language gives you away. Your posture, gestures and tonality reflect your lack of confidence in what you are selling. Clients cannot be expected to see the value in something unless you yourself believe in it. Ask yourself sincerely—would you buy this product for $100?

Now let's look at another case. What if you truly believed that your product was worth a thousand dollars? Would you have difficulty selling it for a hundred? Probably not. You will do it easily, unconsciously communicating to your clients what you think it's worth and will thus meet your goal of increasing your income.

*Whatever you believe in with complete faith and conviction will manifest in your life, whether you want it or you don't.*

A belief is a thought that is absolutely true for you in your world—how you think the world is, how you think people are, and how you think you are. Once you believe something to be true, you get into a state of it being true, till you cannot distinguish between what you believe and what is. They both appear the same.

I have clients who have had a problem for so long that they don't believe it can be solved, and are unable to do so. They might not be aware that it's their conviction in their inability to solve their problem that is keeping them from solving it. Once they believe they can do it, they most likely will.

A person I met a few years ago said to me, "I have to manage my home, my work, and my part-time job. It's too much for me to handle. I don't know how to juggle so many things at once." I asked her if she believed she could do it and she said, "No." It just takes a moment to realize that this belief is stopping her from managing multiple fronts which another person—with different beliefs—might have been able to do.

*You achieve only those things that you think you can. The mind has a need to prove itself right.*

If you keep telling yourself that you are stuck, you will feel that way. Even if solutions are in plain sight, you will not be able to see them because of your belief.

A study was conducted which found that lucky people are lucky because they think of themselves as lucky. When they walked into a room with a ten-dollar bill lying on the floor, they were more likely to spot it than those who thought themselves unlucky.

This has to do with a person's Reticular Activating System (RAS) getting sensitized to a belief. We saw how we filter out certain information in the section on The Filtering Mechanism. The RAS is a bundle of nerves at the brain stem which filters important information. Question is, how does it decide what is *important?*

Important information is subjective to an individual. It depends on the person's map of the world (or unconscious programming). For example, if you are a foodie, you will tend to notice food joints wherever you go— even where others have missed it. If someone asks you for directions, you might direct them with respect to the restaurants in that area. If someone asks you how a wedding was, you might talk about the cake. Similarly, let's say, you recently bought a car which you don't remember seeing on the road. After you buy it, you seem to find it everywhere. The cars were there earlier, but you were not paying attention to them.

*Whatever you focus on appears a lot more in your life because you start filtering information based on it.*

**<u>Confirmation Bias</u>**: If we believe something to be true, we will pay selective attention to it and delete everything else. We unconsciously seek information that validates our belief, not challenges it, because we don't have the brainpower to analyze everything. Hence, the initial input we give ourselves is important because that is what we will most likely get back.

This is also the reason behind recommending staying in an outcome frame while pursuing a goal. We saw in the section on Frames of Thinking that if you focus on solutions, you will find solutions wherever you go and if you look for problems, you will find those too. Since we find them unconsciously, we might not realize that our focus is manifesting them. So, if we keep telling ourselves:

"I don't have enough time."

"I can't have the perfect weight."

"I have poor relationships."

"I am not confident."

We will not have enough time, we will not reach our ideal weight, we will not have the relationships we want or feel confident. We created what we kept affirming to ourselves. It became our self-fulfilling prophecy. Notice how subtly these affirmations reflect our beliefs.

Change the affirmations to:

"I always have time to do what I want to."

"I can achieve my ideal weight."

"I have great relationships."

"I am confident."

(Download the complete list of affirmations recommended for success in the *"Being Yourself Journal"* on romasharma.com)

You might think that just saying these things doesn't make them happen. If I keep saying that I have great relationships, does that mean that the difficult relationships are going to disappear magically? No, they won't. What we are trying to do is create a frame of mind that will help filter information so as to see potential solutions. Once we have built up choices, it will empower us to turn unfavorable situations around.

There was a time when Bob and Susy were happy in their relationship. However, after a few years, things started fizzling out. Susy became resentful of the time Bob was spending with his friends. She craved quality time with him. When the situation didn't change, she started suspecting that he wanted to leave her. She would track him when he went out, snoop in on his messages, and even drop on his conversations, trying to find evidence. Bob tried telling her many times that she is looking for something that isn't there. He assured her of his commitment to their relationship.

This went on for a few months. One day Bob decided that he had had enough. He decided to end the relationship and started thinking of ways to break this to Susy. Susy sensed a change in him. Unfortunately, this time she was right.

Did Suzy predict Bob's leaving? Or did he leave *because* of her prediction? Her firm belief that Bob was planning to break off with her made her behave in ways that pushed him away until finally, he did as she had expected. That is how Suzy manifested the very thing she feared.

Once, when I was teaching two children mathematics, I left a problem statement for the older child and the younger one picked it up. I didn't stop her as she tried to solve it. The next day, much to my surprise, she returned with the correct solution. She was able to solve it because she believed she could. Had I told her that this problem was for the older child, and not for her age group, there is a good chance she would not even have tried! That's how we complete what we picture.

**Exercise**

1. Do you believe you deserve to be successful?
2. Write three reasons why, you believe, you should have the things you want.

# 11

# BELIEFS OF EXCELLENCE FOR SUCCESS

Beliefs are like unquestioned commands to our nervous system. They direct our actions and create our future. It helps to base them on what works well for us and periodically evaluate them for their usefulness.

We have seen that certain beliefs lead to our success while others hold us back. Let's revisit a few we saw while understanding our internal thinking engine. These beliefs have been observed in highly successful people, and adopting them will bring about significant results. Questioning them might delay the process.

**Belief #1:** Each person is unique. The map is not the territory.

**Benefit:** If we were to live this belief, we will not expect people to be exactly like us. We will be more accepting of their uniqueness, improving our relationships.

When we encounter differences with others, we will be able to appreciate that each of us has an unconscious program as unique as our fingerprints, which we use to respond to situations. Hence, their perspective is not *wrong*. The map that they use differs from ours. This belief will help us respect our difference of opinions.

You might have noticed that treating people with respect and appreciation increases the chances of the feeling being reciprocated towards you. Acknowledging that they have a point of view makes them feel understood. It results in deep and meaningful relationships, the foundation for success and helps you establish a rapport with people, undoubtedly your greatest asset.

Rapport gets you co-operation from others. You might run a business, work as a corporate employee, a student, or a parent—irrespective of your role, your ability to get along well with others will decide how far you will go. Think of a person you have a great rapport with. Aren't you ready to do a little extra for that person to succeed?

**Belief #2**: There is no failure. Only feedback.

**Benefit**: If we buy into this belief, we will look at every setback as a learning opportunity.

Failure is *failure* only if you mentally accept it as such. Otherwise, everything is just feedback, helping you do better next time. Think of a few successful people you know. You might notice that they do not identify with the word *failure*. Even when things don't go their way, they create positive interpretations and maintain their resourceful states. This helps them get what they want eventually. Their inner voice does not say, "I failed at doing this." Instead, it says, "I found a way this does not work." They use their results to learn more and get closer to success each time.

When you face a setback, it's essential to be gentle on yourself. Otherwise, you might lose the motivation to try again. Silence the critical inner voice by affirming that your desired results are on their way. You fail to achieve a goal only when you quit or make your results time-bound. For instance, if I want a promotion, I strive towards the goal till I meet it. If I want to get promoted by the end of the day, I might *fail* to do so.

Give yourself time and strategically try different things till you succeed. I don't mean to suggest that deadlines are not important. However, when you don't get the result, would you be willing to give yourself another chance?

Trying again requires careful thought as resources—time, money, and energy—will be spent in the process. If a project is making losses, we don't want to run it relentlessly till we are bankrupt, but at the same time, we don't want to give up on our goals believing that we have failed when success could be right around the corner. It helps to evaluate the results and act accordingly.

Allow yourself to make mistakes. It's okay if the so-called *failure* happened due to decisions you made in the past. There might be some information that you didn't have earlier, which you do now. It's a part of the process that enriches your experience. What is important is to learn from it, try something else, and keep going!

*If every time you fall down you rise more determined, then falling down becomes worth it.*

Accepting that things might go wrong before they go right helps you get into a mindset that is ready to take on challenges. Success is not where you are. Success is everything you overcame to be where you are. When you look at it that way, you will love everything about your goal—roadblocks and challenges included.

**Belief #3**: We already have all the resources we need to be successful.

**Benefit**: Adopting this belief would prevent procrastination. It will be difficult to make excuses for not acting on our goals.

In the section on Well-Defined Outcomes, we saw that we require external and internal resources to achieve goals. Internal resources are in our control and can be leveraged to create external resources. Managing time (an external resource) needs a certain state of mind (an internal resource).

*If we capitalize on our internal resources, we have the power to create any external resource we want.*

We have all heard of people who didn't have the money to eat and lived on the streets, and still created a dream life for themselves. If a person claims to not have time or money, is it the lack of resources or the ability to create them?

Each person has the resources required to be successful in achieving their goals. People who think otherwise don't lack resources, they lack resourcefulness.

**Belief #4**: Every problem has a solution.

**Benefit**: If we believe in this, we will be hopeful of finding solutions even in challenging situations.

As you pursue your goals, unexpected challenges will crop up from time-to-time. If you look for a solution and don't find one, you could experience despair. Your beliefs, at this point, will play an important role in helping you stay hopeful and motivated.

Sometimes, my clients tell me they tried everything but couldn't find a way out of their problem. I hear this a little differently—their desired solution exists but remains unexplored. If they really tried *everything*, they would have found a solution. Maybe their map of the world needs change. Once we work on it and recover information lost through distortion, deletion, and generalization of information, they are likely to discover the solution themselves.

This effort will only be put in if the person believes that a solution exists. Would you dig a well if you knew that you will not find any water? If you believed that the water exists and it's only a matter of time before you find it, you will attempt wholeheartedly.

**Belief #5**: If one person can do it, anybody can do it.

**Benefit**: If we believe in this, our goal will feel achievable to us.

This belief is based on the concept of modelling. If we can find one person who has achieved our goal, it indicates that it is possible for us too. We are not trying to compare ourselves to other people or make ourselves feel less than them. The intention is to find a proof-of-concept which will strengthen our belief in our goal.

If I want to become a successful trainer, I need to start with defining what *success* means to me. Let's say, I want to train 1000 people and receive 80% positive feedback by the end of March next year. I can find a person who has achieved this goal and observe what she did and believed. If I emulate her, there is a good chance that I will get similar results. I also need to ensure I model only that behavior which worked well for her. For example, if she smokes to relieve stress, I might not want to do the same.

It helps to select a model whose ecological conditions are like yours. For instance, a lady who is managing two children and a part-time business might benefit from modeling a person who successfully achieved a similar goal under similar conditions. When I say this, sometimes my clients ask, "What if I cannot find a single person who has achieved what I want to *and* has conditions similar to mine?" In my practice, I have rarely seen such a thing happen. Invariably, you find someone whom you can model. If you are in a niche area, you might have to look a little harder, but the reference does exist.

**Exercise**

1. Which of the beliefs discussed above do you connect with the most?

2. If you were to follow these beliefs, how would it change things for you?

3. Pick a problem you are facing in your life currently, or an area where you would like better results. See if applying one of these beliefs can help you make a breakthrough.

You might already hold some of these beliefs while others might be new to you. You can see which ones you would like to adopt—the more the better. Try new beliefs on for size, and keep them if they fit you well.

In the next section, we will examine an important ingredient required for success, besides beliefs.

# 12

# THE SUCCESS CYCLE

What makes a person successful—intelligence, smartness, or technical know-how? We all know people who have these qualities but are unable to generate the results they want. This usually happens when people do not believe in their own abilities. It is like wearing a fragrant perfume and searching all the world for its source. The potential lies within, but the awareness of it doesn't. As a result, the potential cannot be tapped into. For instance, an intelligent person who does not believe in her intelligence might not leverage it.

Successful people have useful beliefs about themselves—what they can achieve, how far they can go, and what resources they possess. They believe they can succeed and that they deserve it. This allows them to take action, filled with certainty, which brings them remarkable results.

*Whatever you want, just believe it is possible. Achieving it will become a lot easier.*

It is important to note that beliefs on their own don't bring results. We saw in the section on Logical Levels that believing something is possible does not mean we will do anything about it. Great beliefs need to be backed by actions to create results.

*Every grain of rice has the potential to feed the hungry. Potential does not cook the rice.*

There are people who set goals, believe in it wholeheartedly, and do nothing about it. They think about their goals. Then they think about their thinking. Then they think some more. This results in analysis paralysis. The goal is not met because the action was never taken.

We know which books we want to read, but are we reading them? We know how to manage our weight better, but are we doing it? The way to bridge the gap between knowing and doing is by acting. Sometimes we just need a push—to stop overthinking and take that first step!

We see a person who can bench press heavy weights and think that her strength enables her to do it. Actually, it's the other way around. She lifted heavy weights and developed her strength. People might believe that a person is able to manage her house well, excel at her job, and take care of her children because she is smart. Whereas she just kept at it till eventually she became smart at them. Hence, it is the action that gets the result, which further strengthens the action.

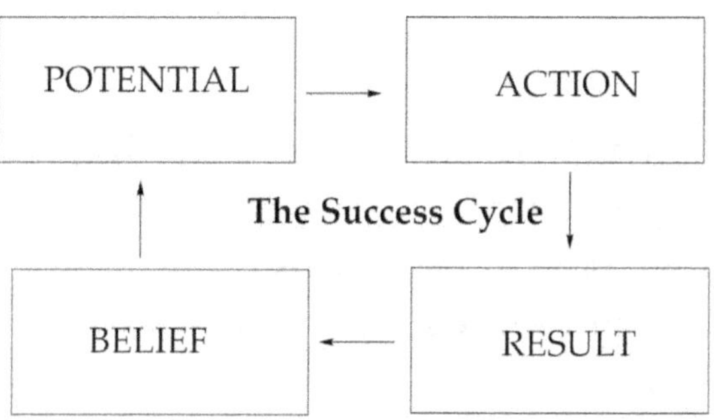


Your beliefs will drive the amount of action you take. If you strongly believe in your potential, you will take massive action towards your goal, which will increase the possibility of getting significant results. When you see these results, it will further strengthen your belief in your potential. On the other hand, if you were doubtful about your success, you will take very little action, see very little result, and prove to yourself that you were right in doubting your success. Your mind will complete whatever it pictures (as we saw in the Self-Fulfilling Prophecy).

The more proof you see in the form of results, the stronger your initial belief becomes. This is how the model creates a powerful loop that ultimately reinforces itself.

**Exercise**

Pick a goal that is not getting you the results you want. Use the Success Cycle to identify the area that needs work:

1. **Potential**: What are your core strengths? Is your goal in line with your potential?
2. **Action**: Have you taken massive action towards your goal? Is there something more you can do?
3. **Beliefs**: Do you believe you can achieve your goal? What are some other beliefs you have around your goal?
4. **Result**: Do your results reflect your beliefs?

**13**

---

# 4-STEP SUCCESS MANTRA

Results are always there, whether we want them or not. The question is—how can we create a lot more of the results that we want?

Here is a 4-Step Success Mantra that has consistently worked for my clients for years. It helps in refining strategies, enabling them to get better results with each iteration. It works well in diverse outcomes—be it in improving relationships or chasing professional goals.

One thing that stands out about this mantra is its simplicity. We don't need much to get better results— just observational skills and a willingness to change.

## Step 1: Define your Goal

A crystal-clear definition of the goal is the first step. Sometimes we say,

"I want to make it in life."

"I want to be happier."

"I want good relationships with everybody."

Our mind doesn't understand panoramic goals because they are unclear—a relationship with whom? By when? How do you define a good relationship? How will you know that you have got it?

*When the goal is ambiguous, the result is ambiguous too.*

Sometimes people tell themselves, "I want to take a break," repeatedly till they fall sick and they finally get a break. Was that the kind of break they were looking for? Probably not. This happens because our unconscious mind is very sensitive to our thoughts. It needs clarity to get us what we want, the way we want it. Once it is programmed accurately, it becomes easy to do.

(Please refer to the section on Well-Defined Outcomes to define your goal clearly.)

**Step 2: Act**

After we have defined our goal, we need to stop thinking and start working. The *planner* in us needs to take a break, and the *doer* needs to be activated. Sometimes, the fact that we are mentally occupied with our goal makes us feel like we are doing something about it while we are just wishing for things. It would be like me chanting, 'Muffins, muffins,' and hoping that somebody comes up to me and says, "Hey Roma, do you want a muffin?" That almost never happens.

If I want a muffin, I have to start with finding a bakery that sells muffins, arrange for the money, go there and make a purchase. Alternately, I can bake it myself. I might face challenges like a long queue at the bakery or the lack of ingredients if I choose to bake one. That will be the extra effort I need to put in to get a muffin. Either way, I had to act to get it. It did not happen to me.

*A goal without a plan is just a wish. A plan with no action is a wish too.*

There can be various reasons for not acting on our goals. Maybe we are scared of the uncertainty. Or maybe we have set high standards for ourselves and the need for perfection prevents us from taking any action. We will address these cases in the upcoming section on Dealing with Procrastination.

**Step 3: Develop Sensory Acuity**

Sensory acuity is your ability to pay attention to what you see, hear, and feel. You need to observe the results of your actions, otherwise you could get caught up in executing your plan and overlook your results. Check with yourself-

Are your actions getting you what you want?

Are they moving you towards your goals or are they just keeping you busy?

Are they in line with the destiny you have chosen for yourself?

Besides evaluating the results of defined goals, it helps to observe the current environment. For instance, when I conduct a training program, I pay attention to the body language of my trainees, for feedback. If they have had a long day at work and are too tired to attend the program, I try to make things interesting by introducing gamification, conducting exercises to help them understand concepts while having fun. Improvisation is possible only with awareness. If I am not paying attention to what I see, hear, and feel around me, I will not be able to meet the outcome of training them well.

*In an outcome frame, observation skills need to be intentionally sharpened to evaluate the quality of the results.*

**Step 4: Be Flexible**

Once you observe what works, you need to act on those observations otherwise developing sensory acuity isn't useful. If you keep doing the same thing, you will keep getting the same result. If something is not working— or can be done better—change your approach. Try something different. It might take a few iterations to fine-tune your approach, but it will eventually get you the result you want. Check with yourself-

What is working well?

What can be done better?

*Do more of what works and less of what doesn't work. Wash - Rinse - Repeat.*

People who cannot demonstrate flexibility find it hard to improve their results. They remain stuck in their old ways long after they have stopped working for them. By being flexible, they can create more choices for themselves and hence be more in control of situations.

Stephanie found her manager, Richard, to be a very demanding person. He would call her to work on weekends and expect her to work remotely on holidays. She was overloaded and stressed. One day, she broke down and realized she couldn't take it anymore. She spoke to her trusted friend and colleague, Phil, to find a way out of this problem.

Phil observed that Stephanie's goal was unclear. She did not know exactly what she wanted, only what she didn't want. He asked her to state what she wants in positive terms. (Changing her blame frame to an outcome frame.)

Stephanie said that she wants a compassionate manager who understood her difficulties and gave her space. She went on to define by when she would like to meet her goal and how she would know that it has been met. The goal was defined, it was time to act on it.

Phil pointed out that Stephanie did not get results earlier because she never tried to communicate her problems to Richard. Stephanie agreed. As part of her action plan, she spoke to Richard about her issues. Luckily, he understood, backed off and gave her more freedom to work. She got what she was looking for, so she did not have to try anything else.

Let's look at the case if Stephanie had not received the desired response. What if Richard became angry and even more controlling? In that case, she would have to demonstrate behavioral flexibility and try something else. Maybe communicate more assertively or approach someone who can mediate the change.

If she tries out different strategies, she will get different results, until she finds one that works. This might even lead to her taking up a new job, which is ok. The outcome is to work with a good manager. There can be many routes that lead to that.

If you are unable to get through to someone, you can try a different style of communicating. For this, you will need behavioral flexibility. If you adapt too easily, you might need to become more assertive. If you are assertive, you might need to reduce it. The same style of communicating might not work across distinct personality types. The key is to try out different things strategically till something works. This requires time, effort, and patience, but is one of the best ways to arrive at a solution.

People who have rigid maps of the world project their maps onto others, getting frustrated when they don't respond as expected. Their inability to adapt to the maps of others leads to strained relationships. Demonstrating flexibility helps in establishing a rapport and facilitates better results.

Flexibility is not only in communication but also in other actions taken towards the goal. Nick's example helps us understand this better.

Nick left his job to become an entrepreneur two years ago. He had been working very hard, but his venture was unfortunately not making any profit. He was too busy to stop and check the direction in which it was heading.

When his money got sucked into projects that gave him no returns, he put more money into them, hoping that they would turn profitable in the next cycle. A few months down the line, Nick was in debt. He could not sustain his operations anymore. He cut down his staff, moved to a smaller office space, and started asking his patrons to loan him some money.

Nick finally got money from a banker at a steep interest rate. The years of effort he had put into his company made him want to give it his best shot. While this was a good idea, what he did not realize was that his *best shot* was not giving him the money he needed. The money was getting drained and, without sealing that hole, he continued pouring water into his bucket of projects.

Soon, he ran out of funds again. Being neck-deep in debt made it difficult for him to support his employees. He let them all go and looked for other avenues for funding. No one was ready to invest in his company because he had the reputation of being careless with money. Eventually, he had to shut his company down.

If Nick were to apply the 4-Step Success Mantra, he would realize that his actions are not helping him make any money. This would be clear in Step 3, where the results are evaluated to check the effectiveness of the actions taken. Once they are flagged as unprofitable, he will take new action in Step 4, depending on his business. He can investigate how his successful competitors are getting excellent results and emulate them. He can also do a cost-benefit analysis of an innovative, low-risk idea that seems to have great potential. (When risks are high, experiments are best carried out by incrementally introducing changes and closely monitoring the results.)

Nick kept working harder and putting more money into his projects. If more time or money was the solution, it would have been evident the first time around. Doing it repeatedly indicates that he was not observant of the results. Strategically trying out something different could have helped him stay afloat.

**Exercise**

Pick an area of life where you want better results. Answer the following questions:

1. Is your goal clearly defined? (Refer: Well-Defined Outcomes)
2. What actions have you taken on this goal?
3. Is your result aligned with your outcome?
4. What will you do more of? What will you do differently?

**14**

---

# DEALING WITH PROCRASTINATION

Lack of motivation is usually a lack of desire to do an activity. This results in postponing the activity which we call procrastination. Procrastination is neurology's way of protecting us. We fear that if a certain job does not get us the intended result, we will go through pain. Hence, our protective unconscious mind ensures we don't start at all.

The underlying reason for trying to escape doing something could be anxiety over the results, fear of failure, confusion, lack of skills, an expectation of perfection etc., based on individual thought patterns. Let's look at some common reasons for procrastination and how to deal with them.

## Pain-Pleasure

We saw in the section on Changing Mindsets that we naturally gravitate towards things that we find pleasurable. If watching a movie gives you more pleasure than doing the dishes, you might avoid doing the dishes and come up with creative reasons for watching a movie. This reasoning—although done skillfully—causes psychological strain because at one level you want to do it, and at another you are unable to. The mind experiences dissonance because what you are thinking and doing are not in sync.

If there is a task you have been postponing for a while, link pleasure to doing it. Imagine all the good things that will happen as a result of completing the task. There are times when the blame frame is useful as well, especially if your goal is based on a *moving-away-from* value. (See section on Values and Beliefs, in Logical Levels)

Imagining the worst-case scenario can help you leverage the blame frame to move you towards your outcome. When you think about the pain of not taking an action, you feel motivated to act on it. While this does work for the *moving-away-from* value, it is still recommended to focus more on the benefits of doing something rather than the downside of not doing it. Holding images of things you don't want—over a period of time—could make those things appear in your life. Program your unconscious mind with excitement over possibilities while moderately using the blame frame, if it helps you motivate yourself.

When you are working towards an outcome, have small rewards built into the system. While extrinsic rewards are useful, it is important to keep the balance firmly in favor of intrinsic rewards—the satisfaction of doing a job well for your own reasons. Rewarding yourself will increase the pleasure you experience in carrying out your activities, helping you stay motivated.

## Anxiety

Procrastination is sometimes laced with anxiety, keeping the person from doing a job without considering the benefit that might come from doing it. Anxiety is good in small amounts. It's a signal from the body that something important is about to happen and you need to be prepared for it. However, it becomes a problem if it paralyzes you and prevents you from acting on your plans.

### 1. A Goal too Big

If your goal is aggressive, taking the first step could feel overwhelming. Let's say you find the thought of climbing up a mountain intimidating. If you want to do it, you can think about the intermediate points along the journey and the amazing view you will find when you reach. That will get you excited. Your goal is now compelling. We have chunked it down into easy, action-able steps, which I also like to call *baby steps*.

Find the first, smallest thing you can do towards achieving your goal. The step should feel safe. *Safe* is something you can easily visualize yourself doing. Instead of trying to reach the peak of the mountain, set yourself up to reach the first base station.

Identify the first baby step and act on it immediately. Follow that action with another and keep going. Every time you succeed in a baby step, your natural motivation will take over and your actions will build up. You will soon create momentum that is hard to stop.

*Action isn't just the effect of motivation. It is also the cause of it.*

Give yourself positive reinforcement by congratulating yourself immediately after achieving a baby step. A simple act of appreciation goes a long way in creating a positive feed forward loop. You want that good feeling again, and are more likely to continue working on your goal.

In the section Thinking is a Habit, we saw that things are difficult only the first time they are done. The second time you have proof-of-concept. You also have neural pathways inside your brain for that behavior. If you can engage in a behavior even once, you've got something to build on. What is the first step you can take towards your goal? Can you do it now?

## 2. Suppressed Excitement

People think a person who is procrastinating is lazy. This might not be the case. Sometimes, the unconscious mind is scared—like a little child—and looks for ways to escape. The fear of going *wrong* keeps us from taking the first step, and we procrastinate.

*If we do nothing, we can't go wrong. Unfortunately, we can't go right either.*

Fritz Perls, the founder of Gestalt Therapy, said that anxiety is suppressed excitement. It happens when our excitement isn't able to flow into the environment freely, perhaps because of the uncertainty around the results our actions will bring—bouquets or brickbats? This thought causes us to hesitate, and we become anxious.

If you ever feel this way, change the mental movie you are playing. Instead of getting scared about the problems you might face, get excited about all the great things that are going to happen. This thought will allow your energy to flow out naturally into the environment and cause your best performance.

## 3. What If

People who fear failure often think that courageous people aren't fearful. Being courageous is not the absence of fear. It is about doing what needs to be done despite it.

Conquer the toughest goal in your life. Nothing will seem impossible anymore. In my coaching sessions, my clients ask me, "What if I fail?" My usual response is, "What if you don't?" After a moment of silence, they smile.

The **what if** game is based on imagination and imagination knows no bounds. We can endlessly guess potential outcomes and not arrive at anything useful. If we must wonder **what if**, I would like to know-

What if you could have everything you ever wished for?

What if you went further than you expected?

When people doubt themselves, they do so with confidence, indicating that they have the capacity to generate confidence. When my clients doubt themselves, I get them to doubt their confidence. To get through to them, I need to be confident. I have sufficient evidence from my practice that people can achieve practically *anything* they set out to. This belief gets conveyed to them, and it gets me the results I am looking for. (If you are working as a coach and don't believe in your client's success, end the professional relationship. Otherwise, it will be a disservice to your client and to yourself.)

## Confusion

We don't like to be confused. Not knowing what will happen can be disorienting. The uncertainty prevents us from acting on our goals. Here are some examples of confusing thoughts that could lead to procrastination-

"I don't know what to do next."

"What will happen if I do this and it doesn't work out?"

"What will I be missing out on?"

"Will I regret this later?"

These thoughts can leave us second guessing because there is no way for us to know this at present.

You might feel confused when you have too many options or do not have the required skills to make an informed choice. Here, remember that when you have a goal in mind; you don't have to know anything about it in advance. You just need to be committed to finding out. When you say, "I don't know," you have reached the limit of the model of your world. If you relentlessly seek answers to your questions, you will ultimately find what you are looking for.

*It's good to be confused. Confusion is the doorway to new understanding.*

If you have been trying too hard to ease a state of confusion with little luck, then pause thinking about it. You might need to deal with the urgency of knowing things. When water is muddy, it's best to let it stand still. Give it some time. The mud will settle down and the water will be clear again. This does not mean that we should be inactive. It just means that with time and patience, confusion will bring clarity. It is also a way to allow better things into our life. More so, if we can see it that way.

(If your confusion is concerning an important decision, and it persists over time, you might need to check if your goal is aligned with your values. When values are clear, it becomes easy to decide. Persistent confusion could indicate a value-misalignment.)

## Perfectionism

Perfectionism is about wanting things to be perfect as per one's standards. It is about holding an image inside the mind and expecting external situations to match up. The mental image is rigid. Life, on the other hand, changes from one moment to another—sometimes drastically. Occurrences in the world might not fit well with the mental image. This mismatch causes frustration in the mind of the perfectionist. (If you call yourself that, you might need to revise your identity statement.)

The perfect image held inside the mind is not *perfect*. If

it was, it would be flexible and would adapt to situations. It would provide more options and allow us to pick the best one.

Perfectionism is not a desirable quality, as some might think. It is usually an area of work. Desiring perfection can make a person controlling and obsessive. It can cause disappointment when things don't go as expected. It creates pressure due to unrealistic expectations of flawlessness—from oneself and others. This could cause procrastination, putting dream projects off waiting for the situation to be perfect. You might have heard statements such as-

"I will start my business when my kids grow up."

"I will earn more money when I find the perfect job."

"I will start exercising regularly when I have more time."

The best time to work on your goals is *now*. Situations are rarely ever going to be perfect. Things might get better or worse in the future. Either way, you will have a head start on your goals. There could be concerns over how your goal will impact your ecology or how you will arrange for the required resources. However, once you have checked your goal with respect to the factors discussed in Well-Defined Outcomes, those areas would have been addressed. Act on your well-formed goal immediately and unfavorable situations will adapt, like water that flows over the rocks.

It's good to set high standards for yourself, but sometimes that can deter your progress. If you have been pondering over the *best way* to do something, maybe it's time to just *do something* and see where it gets you. Fine-tune your approach and try again.

I dealt with my expectations of perfection a few years ago. I was designing a new program, and I wanted everything to go right. That caused me to sit on the project for months. I thought I was working hard on it, which was a skillfully designed cover for delaying the launch. My mentor pointed this out to me. He said, "It is very difficult to know all probable outcomes in advance. You just need to do what you think will work, allow yourself to make mistakes, and take what comes next."

I was amazed at how fast he had caught the underlying problem. I implemented his advice and got my results. The program was launched successfully and evolved over time to meet the requirements of the trainees well.

It is important to note that not all jobs require perfection. They just need to be done moderately well. For instance, if I need to create a plan for the activities of the week, I don't need to have perfectly shaped columns, calligraphic designs, and colorful notes. I can simply jot down the tasks which I can strike out, once complete. Time saved from beautifying the timetable can be better utilized.

If you identify an activity being done more perfectly than required, set a time limit to it and strive towards finishing it in the allotted time. Remind yourself that it just needs to be done. Doing it perfectly will take time away from other activities. Keeping yourself busy with an unimportant activity is also a way of procrastinating.

Sometimes people spend time on the frill because they don't want to do the drill. The reason behind setting up an escape route is usually a lack of desire to do the activity. It is important to address the underlying feeling causing this behavior. The reason could be as simple as needing a break, in which case, you can plan some downtime and return to your work later, rejuvenated.

**Exercise**

1. Think of an activity that is important for achieving your goal, but you have been postponing for a while.
2. Write what you will get by successfully doing that activity.
3. Write what you will miss out on if you were to put that activity off for later.
4. Close your eyes and imagine yourself doing that activity all the way to the moment of completion.
5. Imagine the same sequence again, this time looking at it through your own eyes.

15
—————

# FEELING STATES FOR SUCCESS

The starting point for success is feelings. We saw that what a person needs to feel to succeed is subjective. However, there are some states known to help most people succeed in their endeavors. Let's go over them. You might already have some of these states and want to include others. Just like beliefs, you can try them on and see if they work for you.

## Awareness

Managing feeling states starts with awareness. If you are aware that you are stressed, you can distance yourself from the trigger and calm down. However, if you are unaware, your state might spin out of control, alerting you of the condition only when it's too late.

The best way to be aware of your feelings is to observe your body because all feelings manifest somewhere in the body. For instance, if your breath is shallow and the muscles around the neck feel tight, it indicates that you are stressed. Similarly, if you are anxious you might experience palpitations, sweaty palms, dryness of throat, etc. Being in touch with your feelings helps you take care of them at the right time.

Awareness is not limited to your mind and body. When an outcome is linked to your actions, it is important to be aware of what you see, hear, and feel in the external environment as well. Developing sensory acuity (see Step 3 in 4-Step Success Mantra) can help you incrementally improve on your results.

## Openness & Flexibility

Being open to change helps us improve. Openness can be developed by appreciating different perspectives. People who reject any thoughts on self-improvement, personally or professionally, limit their scope of growth. It is ok to take feedback so as to improve. What is not ok is for us to beat ourselves up over it.

To work on the feedback received from your environment, you need to demonstrate flexibility. Otherwise, the feedback isn't of much use. With minimum risk, try to do things differently and notice how comfortable you are. Just like physical exercise, stretching a little every day will gradually enhance mental flexibility.

Being flexible will help you adapt to situations quickly and land on your feet every time. You will be able to adjust to different people, making it easy for you to develop a rapport with others, and be influential. Hence, being open and flexible gives you more control over situations.

## Relentlessness & Commitment

Relentlessness is the single most distinguishing quality of successful people. They are comfortable with things not working out. They accept setbacks as a part of the process, learn what they can, and try again.

When faced with adversity, people tend to give up. They change direction or switch to something easier when they could be only a few steps away from success. The ones who are determined even when it rains on their parade ultimately succeed.

Being determined comes from being committed to a goal, which differs from being attached to it. Attachment to a goal can cause misery when the result is not as expected. The fear of going wrong can prevent a person from taking action. A baby who is learning to live in this world needs to be taken care of when she cries, needs food, or can't sleep. She will settle down in a matter of time, but before that she needs a person who is committed to the process. If her caretaker is attached to her, it might cause disappointment over her difficulties, which might not be useful to her. The baby needs commitment over attachment.

Likewise, when you are working towards a goal, the return is in the future but the difficulties are in the present, such as confusion, uncertainty, tiredness, and frustration. If you are committed to dealing with them, you will get the returns you are looking for.

*Your ability to do something you don't feel like doing will determine the amount of success you will achieve in any endeavor. There will be a test.*

I hear people say that they want a good relationship with a certain person. Their attempts to improve the relationship start well. However, when they face contention, they go back to their old ways of reacting.

Hoping for a better relationship does not get us one. It requires commitment to do what needs to be done—communicate well, ask for what we need, and understand others' viewpoint. This is work. If you want a better relationship with someone, ask yourself, "Am I willing to do what it takes to have one?" The answer to this question will indicate your level of determination.

Irrespective of which area your goal belongs to—be it relationships, business, or fitness—your determination will be a factor of how strong your desire is and what you are willing to do for it. Can you last through the rough days that threaten to overpower your determination?

You need daily motivation to do your work. During crises, you need more of it. This is when the gradient of challenge is no longer a slope; it becomes vertical. When faced with such situations, pause and ask yourself-

"How can I turn this around?"

"What is not perfect yet?"

"What am I willing to do to make things the way I want them to be?"

"What can I learn from this?"

"How can I enjoy the process of taking the required actions?"

Once you have sufficient clarity, get back into action-mode. Asking questions beyond a point can lead to uncertainty.

(Follow the 4-Step Success Mantra to stay on track. We want to be relentless, but not without reason. Determination without direction can be quite risky.)

## Pragmatism & Responsibility

Pragmatism is the attitude of doing the smartest thing in any situation. When faced with problems, pragmatic people try to find the best potential solution. They are sensitive to their environment and proactively evaluate the information available to assess their results. Even in the absence of problems, they look for practical and logical methods to do things. They enter an outcome frame by asking themselves, "What is the most useful thing to do right now?"

People who demonstrate responsibility have the ability to respond, rather than react, to situations. When things go wrong, they don't waste time blaming others, trying to control them, or feeling sorry for themselves. Instead, they take responsibility by focusing on what they can do.

Being responsible and pragmatic automatically switches people from a blame frame to an outcome frame. It puts them in charge of their results as the power lies with them. Having such a power can be quite liberating.

## Playfulness & Curiosity

Curiosity is a great learning state. The more curious you are, the more questions you ask which will enhance your knowledge. A strong desire to learn something makes a person naturally curious. Have you seen how knowledgeable people are in the area they are passionate about? They can talk in depth and give you more details on the subject than you could ask for. Their interest keeps them seeking and learning.

Playfulness is a great learning state too. Do you remember being playful when you were a child? That was the time when you learned a lot. This is one reason a child's grasping power is higher than an average adults. Not because the learning ability reduces with age, but because people start taking themselves and the world too seriously. They create beliefs that deter them from learning, for instance, "I am too old to learn anything new." If we could be in a lighter and more playful mood, we would learn unconsciously.

Being playful and curious also increases your creativity. Have you noticed how children sometimes give out-of-the-box solutions, which leave us dazed and amused? Connect with your inner child to return to the states in which your creativity flows naturally. It helps in finding innovative solutions to problems.

**Exercise**

1. The following exercise is done to improve the states of openness and flexibility.
2. Pick a point of contention between you and another person.
3. Write an argument imagining yourself to be the other person.
4. Take a brief break and read what you have written.
5. Answer the following questions:

- What did you learn about the person's viewpoint?
- Is there something you can do differently to elicit a different response from this person?

# 16

# HOW TO CHANGE YOUR HABITS OF THINKING

If you want to change a habit of thinking it is important to change what you are doing with your time. If you can sustain a new pattern of behavior for just 40 days, it will become a part of your unconscious process.

*You become whatever you keep doing.*

Let's look at some things that can be done to change our thinking habits. The list might seem long, but everything does not need to be done at once. You can pick a few of the suggested methods. After you have successfully incorporated them into your daily routine, pick another. The more methods you can adopt, the better results you will get.

1. Journal your thoughts daily. Set a time aside to write anything that comes to your mind. Read your journal regularly. Scan it for underlying beliefs that might limit your progress. For example, thoughts like, "I don't

think I will ever be able to solve this," reflect a feeling of despair and indicate a belief that might need change. Make a note of these beliefs and challenge them using the Belief Change Table provided in the section on Source of Beliefs. You can also do the exercise provided in the section on Beliefs of Excellence for Success.

Read your journal in a different frame of mind to understand your feelings better. Feelings don't need to be challenged. They need to be understood. If your feelings are preventing you from achieving your goals, meditation and coaching will help.

2. Meditate for 20 minutes in silence every day. Set a space and time aside for this activity. The energy of that space will help you go into a meditative state faster. Observe your thoughts without trying to control them, focus on your breath, and tap into your inner calmness to rejuvenate your mind and body. Meditation will change your filtering mechanism to focus on things that help you maintain the relaxed state. This will also improve your relationships and enhance your efficiency at work.

3. Spend time with people who have already achieved what you want to. Connect with them over groups, online or face-to-face. Keep in touch with them and learn from them. Join or create a group of people who have goals similar to yours—preferably around the same stage of achieving them. Besides having technical

know-how, they will understand your struggles and are likely to support you.

Set a cap on the time spent in these groups, especially if they are online. This helps in utilizing time together for exchanging information. Learn from the ones who know and teach the ones who might benefit from your knowledge. There is immense value in grouping together because the whole is greater than the sum of its parts.

4. Avoid people who don't believe in your success, who are pessimistic, or talk more about problems rather than solutions. Their negative thinking will seep into your unconscious mind and create self-doubt. Avoid taking advice from people who don't understand your work or have never pushed themselves out of their comfort zone.

When you say *yes* to something, you say *no* to something else. Spend your time judiciously by saying *no* to people who can't create results or tell you that you can't. There are many reasons why something can't be done. We are looking for ways in which it can.

5. Spend time by yourself every day. Use this time to introspect the overall direction in which you are headed. Step out of your role and look at yourself from a disassociated view. Encourage yourself. Review your plan for what can be done better.

Digital technology has become invasive with its notifications and pop-ups, distracting us from spending quality time with anyone, including ourselves. Have you noticed that if people are left alone—even for a short while—they start browsing their phones? People who identify with this need to remember that no notification informs us that we missed connecting with ourselves. There is value in spending time away from worldly distractions and evaluating our progress.

6. Train your unconscious mind with visualizations and positive affirmations. Consciously spend 10 minutes every day visualizing the amazing things that will happen when your goals are achieved. How will it benefit you? What will it do for others?

Write positive affirmations that support your goals and read them aloud every day. In a few months, they will permeate into your unconscious mind. (Download the complete list of affirmations in the **"Being Yourself Journal"** available on romasharma.com)

7. Self-care is an important—and often neglected—aspect of a goal-oriented life. When your body indicates tiredness, get rest or a massage. Schedule downtime and prioritize it, otherwise, it could cause burnout.

Spend time every day doing something that you are passionate about—singing, dancing, playing sports, etc. When you do what you love to do, it improves your mood and boosts your productivity.

8. Make the time to read every day. Select books, blog posts, or articles. Reading high-quality, inspirational material daily leaves a positive impact on one's unconscious mind. It helps to read the biographies of people who achieved success despite trying conditions. Success stories expand our horizons and inspire us during tough times.

9. Undergo coaching or training if you want professional support. In a coaching session, you can set your goals based on the thinking habits you would like to change. Your coach will work with you towards defining your goal, creating an action plan for it, and helping you stay accountable for your progress. (While this book has provided the most common thinking patterns that can be adopted for success, you might have some specific patterns that you would like to address in a coaching session.)

10. Spend time every day being grateful for three people in your life. Write down what you appreciate about them. You can tell them, if you choose to.

What are some gifts that life has given you? Write three things you are grateful to life for, such as your health, freedom, certain qualities you have.

Thinking about what we have creates an abundance mindset. We feel happy when we focus on our gifts, and our happiness helps create more to be grateful for. It becomes a self-sustaining loop.

Fear results from having faith in the lack of things. Thinking about our blessings helps us deal with this fear. Since many good things have happened with us, it reinforces our faith in more good things to come.

11. Practice the exercises provided at the end of each section in this book. You can refer to Well-Defined Outcomes while setting your goals, or use Logical Levels if you want clarity in a situation. You can use the Frame of Thinking and 4-Step Success Mantra to generate better results. Based on your situation, use the associated self-coaching questions to change your thoughts and enter resourceful states. Do this repeatedly till it becomes an unconscious habit of thinking.

The above methods will significantly enhance your chances of success. Give yourself as much time as you need. The neural pathways that created old thought patterns took time to strengthen. Patience and persistence are required to change them.

If you find yourself in an unresourceful state, take a brief break from your work, journal your thoughts, and put them away. Take a few deep breaths (or meditate, if possible) and return to what you have written. Scan it for blame frames, underlying limiting beliefs, and value conflicts. Switch to an outcome frame—what do you want in this situation? As your thoughts change, your feelings will change too.

If you can stay committed to practicing the suggested methods for changing thought patterns, phenomenal results are definite. I have only listed the methods that have worked well for my clients. Since we have a limited amount of time, it is important to spend it optimally doing only the things that will get us maximum returns.

Sometimes my clients avoid these activities, considering them to be an overload on their already busy schedule. It helps to remember that structuring our time judiciously is the best way to bring about change, like the time spent in sharpening an axe before using it.

*We don't change because of the things we are not willing to do.*

You can find more information on ways to manage feeling states like journaling, coaching, training, and meditation in my book, **"What Will People Think?"**. Please read it to know more about how you can stay calm despite trying situations in the world.

## 17

## AFTERWORD

What will you do after you have achieved your goal? If you don't have a plan, the results will be fleeting. Imagine a person who earned her desired amount of money but didn't plan for after that. She might lose the benefit of her financial gain. If she achieved her fitness goal and didn't think of how she would maintain her fitness, she could lose her rejuvenated health. A goal beyond a goal is required because success is about the overall direction you are heading in—one that is right for you.

Would you like a life in which you are excited to get out of bed every morning? It's possible if you align your strengths with what makes you happy and create your goals around that. When your goals are in line with your desires, you need no motivation. The thought of your day will get you started.

In a goal-oriented mindset, the focus is on getting things done. You also need to cope with the thoughts and feelings that threaten to overwhelm you. Effective management of feelings is a useful skill to have. If I am about to enter an interview room and I feel anxious, I might not present myself in the best way possible. If I want to ask someone out and I fumble, I might not be able to hold a conversation long enough to do so.

*People who feel good about themselves produce excellent results.*

If you ever feel scared to pursue your dreams, remember how fearless you were as a child. You thought you could do anything, till somebody told you that your powers are limited—that you cannot fly off a building like Superman! Their beliefs poured in, limiting yours.

Reclaim your power by recognizing all the challenges you have overcome to be where you are today. Even in the future, life might throw curve balls at you. Situations might not always be favorable. The environment in which you operate might not be conducive to your results. You are not defined by what happens to you. You are defined by how you respond to what happens. Your ability to face challenges will ensure that you meet your goals, increasing as you continue on your chosen path.

Success comes to those who plan for it. Otherwise, even if a person wins a lottery, she will not be able to sustain her results because they were random. When you define your goals, create an action plan, and execute it to the best of your ability, you generate results predictably. It's also important to note that the future is always uncertain. It helps to keep your outcome fluid to an extent. When things don't go as planned, accept the change and adapt to the new situation as soon as possible.

It's good to have goals. Otherwise, one could end up like a ship wrecked because it was sailing without a direction. It's good to work hard to attain those goals, as it gives your confidence a boost. At the same time, driving yourself beyond a point can be stressful.

The balance between a goal-oriented mindset and self-care is delicate. It's easy to get pulled into one and neglect the other. If you work too hard on your goals but suffer from poor health and relationships, we can't call it success. If you take good care of yourself but don't work hard enough on your goals, then you might not be successful either.

Success lies in the balance. It is about the quality of life you live. There are many ways to achieve the things you want. The question is, are you living your core values while doing all this? Are you happy with the person success has made you?

Success is in growth—in being the best version of yourself holistically. The only comparison is with older versions of yourself (and not with others). It doesn't matter how much better others are than you, or what they think about your goal. What matters is doing what you want, for your own reasons, wholeheartedly.

Design a life you would love to live. Believe in yourself like your life depends on it. Commit to your goal and cut yourself off from any other possibility.

To Your Success,

Roma

**Please Review This Book**

We have reached the end of the book and I sincerely hope that you found value in it. I have a request for you. If you liked the book, would you please let others know about it?

1. Please leave a review on an online store that is convenient for you. (If you log onto romasharma.com and click on the book, you will find the list of store-fronts where it is available.)

2. Share it on Facebook, Twitter, Instagram, Pinterest or LinkedIn

3. Please mention it to your circle of family, friends or colleagues

Reviews help readers discover books they like. They are the best way to get the word out. Even a line or two of your views on the book will help.

Thank you for taking the time to do this. Your support is much appreciated. I look forward to reading your views.

# ABOUT THE AUTHOR

Roma Sharma is a Certified Coach and Trainer who has been working in the field of emotional well-being since 2014. She runs a training company that authors programs for people from a variety of backgrounds—IT Industry, Educational Institutions, Counseling Academies, and Hospitality Industry to name a few. She works with organizations to design programs that specifically address their training needs.

Roma has a keen interest in understanding human behavior and connecting with people at a deeper level. Besides training and coaching, she regularly hosts a meetup in her city to discuss various topics related to mental health.

She likes to take up issues that her audience members experience in their day-to-day life and provide them with clarity so that they devise simple solutions that work well for them. She has had the privilege of watching her clients become very successful in attaining the transformation that they set out to achieve.

When she is not training, she loves to bake cakes, read books, and play with cats.

**Credentials:**

- B.E (CSE)
- Diploma in Counselling Skills, person-centered therapy
- International Certification in Transactional Analysis 101
- Foundation course in Transactional Analysis
- Master practitioner of NLP (ABNLP), NLP Trainer
- Advanced Diploma in Hypnosis (Business-NLP, UK)

# STAY IN TOUCH

Here are the best ways to stay in touch with me:

**Subscribe to my Newsletter**

Please leave your mail ID at **romasharma.com/newsletter** to receive articles on the best coaching practices, free video training programs, and eBooks.

**Like my Facebook Page**

Hit the like button on my Author Page **facebook.com/romasharmawriter** to receive the latest news from the world of coaching and the best offers on my new releases.

# DOWNLOAD YOUR FREE 'BEING YOURSELF JOURNAL'

I hope you have downloaded your copy of the journal. If you have not, here it is again.

## Your FREE Book!

For more books log onto
romasharma.com

The Being Yourself Journal with powerful self-coaching questions is available at **romasharma.com**

Here is what you will find in the journal:

1. Page templates you can fill out every day to connect with your thoughts and feelings
2. Affirmations to increase self-esteem and confidence
3. Self-coaching questions that will help you find solutions in difficult situations
4. Simple ways to decrease worry and stay calm in the present moment

Journaling is a powerful way to understand yourself better. The way you feel about your thoughts changes when you write them down. If you journal on a regular basis you will find that—in a matter of time—your journal will become the single most useful document you have on yourself.

Whether you need to find a solution to a problem or just vent out your feelings, your journal is available to you whenever you need it. Download your copy and start journaling today.

**Download now! Log onto romasharma.com**

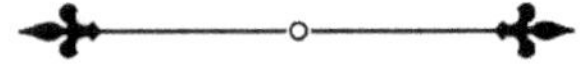